# ENDORSEN

In this moving and informative autobiography, Hyacinth reveals what it means to live in pursuit of a deeper understanding of God. It deserves wide readership by people of faith and no faith.

—Dr. Joe Aldred

Hyacinth's autobiography is informative, miraculous and intriguing. It will definitely keep you turning the pages.

—Lilieth Wade

Hyacinth is a woman of great faith. I have known her from my teenage years. As I read her book, I was able to recapture some of the 'God-moment' testimonies she would share with me on our visits or over the telephone. A very good read!

—Elaine June Easie

An absolutely wonderful and well-written book. It should be read by Christians and non-Christians alike to bring light and clarity to people's lives. I can only reiterate it has been a fantastic read, from start to finish.

—Tony Fraser

*Journey to Wholeness* is a breath of fresh air! Orwell said: *And if all others accepted the lie . . . if all records told the same tale—then the lie passed into history and became truth* (George Orwell, *1984*). As I read *Journey to Wholeness*, I am reminded of the Word: *The earth is given into the hands of the wicked; He covers the faces of its judges [so that they are blind to justice]* (Job 9:24).

Within the pages of her book, Hyacinth literally walks us through Kingdom righteousness being established in the earth (Matthew 6:10). This new writing, from a second generation Caribbean woman, is truly challenging the status quo! The *inclusion* of the *authentic stories*, of the unsung heroes who contributed to the building of this nation, is *widening participation* and altering the complexion of what is accepted as 'good literature' . . . *this generation shall not pass away until all these things be fulfilled.*

—Eulet Davy

Cinth is the evidence and definition of a beautiful woman; a woman of excellence. She does nothing half-heartedly, but with quiet unreserved determination combined with purposeful passion she not only succeeds, but excels in life's challenges. This portrayal of her life is inspired, informative, sometimes humorous and at other times sad. It is a moving and unforgettable account of her journey with vulnerability and transparency. She shares her search for motherhood, the reality of wife and homemaker, combined with career and church, balancing academia and finally health. We see unconditional love and unadulterated commitment for her 'forever family' and others. I thank God He sustained her and restored her health.

In the midst of physical and emotional pain and suffering, she shares miracles and encounters in the supernatural realm. Despite health challenges, racism and discrimination, this woman with her God walks this journey of faith as an overcomer . . . A sequel awaits. . . .

—Eileen Mignott

# JOURNEY TO WHOLENESS

**Also by Hyacinth Fraser**

Formation of One Accord Group
The Way Forward in Christian Education
Region 5 Training and Development Prospectus
Mansfield, Local Church Vision
A Basic Guide to Medical Terminology

# JOURNEY TO WHOLENESS

*10 Steps to Turn Setbacks into Setups*

**HYACINTH WHEELER-FRASER**

Printed in the United States of America
Published by Author Academy Elite, P.O. Box 43, Powell, OH 43035
www.AuthorAcademyElite.com

Paperback: ISBN-978-1-64085-079-8
Hardback: ISBN- 978-1-64085-080-4
EBook: ISBN-978-1-64085-081-1

Library of Congress Control Number: 2017910759
Author Academy Elite, Powell, OH

Unless otherwise indicated, Scripture quotations are from the Holy Bible: Amplified (AMP); Amplified Classic (AMPC); New King James Version (NKJV).

If from the 2015 edition, Scripture quotations are taken from the Amplified® Bible (AMP), Copyright © 2015 by The Lockman Foundation. Used by permission. www.Lockman.org.

If from the 1987 edition: Scripture quotations taken from the Amplified® Bible (AMPC),

Copyright © 1954, 1958, 1962, 1964, 1965, 1987 by The Lockman Foundation. Used by permission. www.Lockman.org.

**Disclaimer**
To protect the privacy of those who have shared their stories with the author, some details and names have been changed.

# CONTENTS

# FOREWORD

'Where is a loving God when you are hurting? How should you respond to the challenges happening in the midst of a crisis? Our uniqueness sets us apart in the way we respond. Either we give up, blame God or are resilient. In the vast majority of humans, there is a natural tendency to find some kind of inner strength to turn our experience of tragedies into triumphs.'

In her autobiography, Hyacinth takes you on a journey to help you find answers. Drawing on the inner strength, she attributes to God, she rises to her challenges and shows how she overcame against the odds.

The launch of *Journey to Wholeness* is borne out of her own health challenges, which she faced several times. She describes these challenges as *déjà vu* moments. Time after time, she found herself standing at the same crossroad, where she would make life changing decisions. Structured into several different journeys and written optimistically, she takes you through the emotional roller coaster of the highs and lows of the journey, from sickness and despair to healing, wellness, and restoration.

Hyacinth is a great storyteller who captures the imagination. Her vulnerable approach will help you to resonate with her resilience and the unconditional love she has for her children, even when those closest to her don't understand.

At the heart of her book is the step-by-step approach used in her subtitle as: 10 steps to turn setbacks into setups. She provides useful tips on specific themes around self-discovery; walking through the process; playing to your strength; abiding in His presence and celebrating your new season.

Reading this book is a step in the right direction to identifying your God-given purpose and destiny.

Her book will resonate with a universal audience as the topics and issues she touches on (e.g. decision making in the judicial and care systems) affect families and carers, communities, and society on a whole.

I know you will enjoy the ride and learn from the lessons called LIFE.

Kary Oberbrunner
Author of: ELIXIR Project; Day Job to Dream Job;
The Deeper Path and Your Secret Name.

# ACKNOWLEDGEMENTS

## Heavenly Father

You are my Source, Life and Salvation. I give You the highest praise. I couldn't have completed this book without You. Finding intimacy and relationship in the secret place, has given me insight and revelation of who You are. Father, You exceed my highest expectations, dreams and imaginations. You ARE my GOD.

## Family

I am grateful to my husband and soul mate, Tony. You have consistently encouraged and urged me to write and faithfully supported me over the years. To my precious children, Jenny and Jason, thank you for contributing to my book. My siblings, Eileen (best friend), Peter, Rosemarie, Samuel, Clement and Marina have encouraged and inspired me in the different seasons of my life. To my parents, Archibald Washington and Clarissa Lovina; my brother Samuel and brother-in-law Verley, now in heaven, I thank God for you all, especially during the highs and lows of my life. Individually, you have challenged me to rise above my limitations and to soar high, like an eagle.

## Coach—Kary Oberbrunner

I was excited by the prospect of writing my story. Thank you, Kary, for believing in me. You have motivated me to the degree where I am growing in writing. You have given me some incredible tools to use. Your mentorship, patience and prayers have been invaluable and a great blessing.

## Friends

I am thankful to Eileen Mignott, Lilieth Wade, Bishop Dr. Joe Aldred, Norman Wright, John Hoffman, Elaine June Easie and Eulet Davy, to name a few, for your friendship, support and contribution to my book.

# DAWNING OF A NEW ERA

## Part 1—Introduction

In tragedy, we seek for answers and we find ways to rationalise our experience. In those times, the most fundamental questions of existence are repeatedly raised.

In the Bible, Job asks, "What is man?" For me, the question was, "How did this happen?"

Our uniqueness sets us apart in the way we respond. Either we give up, blame God, or are resilient. In the vast majority of humans, there is a natural tendency to find some kind of inner strength to turn our experience of tragedies into triumphs.

The Apostle Paul wrote *"And we know [with great confidence] that God [who is deeply concerned about us] causes all things to work together [as a plan] for good for those who love God, to those who are called according to His plan and purpose"* (Romans 8:28).

He also wrote *"But thanks be to God, who always leads us in triumph in Christ, and through us spreads and makes evident everywhere the sweet fragrance of the knowledge of Him"* (2 Corinthians 2:14). I'm a great believer that the Father always, *always* being the operative word, causes us to triumph over our adversities.

Holding on to bitterness prevents us from moving forward and living prosperous lives. In fact, people who overcome personal tragedies look for ways to help others. Imagine losing a child, then campaigning to reform a system of inequalities in our nation?

When calamity strikes suddenly, how is it possible to say, "I forgive?" I have discovered that our greatest successes and triumphs are borne out of pain, tears and sweat. The description used by Daystar's Christian television captures the meaning of my journey beautifully:

*A journey shows us not only the world but our purpose in it; painted by our passion, our struggle, our beliefs, the journey brings us face to face with ourselves, our relationships and our God* (Justin Machacek 2010).

When I received the news of my breast cancer in 2005, it was the first of three diagnoses. After surgery and without chemotherapy, I made a full recovery by God's healing power. At that time, I felt the urge to write my autobiography and memoir. Although the route was not one I would have chosen (the journey was a long process, a 'walking through' experience rather than an instant miracle), Father God guided me every step of the way.

On numerous occasions, I felt I was being carried in His arms, as described in the poem: *Footprints*. The story describes an experience in which a man is walking on a beach with God. Together, they leave two sets of footprints in the sand behind them. The journey represents various stages of the man's life. Looking back at significant points, he notices where the two sets of footprints dwindle to one. At the times he felt were the lowest and most hopeless moments of his life, he sees only one set of footprints. Believing that the Lord must have abandoned him during those times, he questions God. The Father explains: "During your times of trial and suffering, when you see only one set of footprints, it was then that I carried you." (Wikipedia n.d.).

Recovering from major reconstructive surgery, I was struck down with a long episode of insomnia, lasting an entire year. Still valiantly staying the course, as wife and mother, I eventually returned to work and to even more 'urgent and important' tasks after that year.

These included juggling the different roles of student, pastor, and director of a company. It all became too much, and I didn't get very far with writing. Added to our busy life, my husband and I began another stressful journey with the Social Care system. There were peaks and troughs as we battled for the right services for our children.

The experience was like 'fire fighting' without any real solution. Once again, my writing took a back seat, and got further out of my reach. In 2012, I was diagnosed with cancer for the second time.

There was bloatedness in my stomach and swelling all over my body. I knew that something was wrong. I was misdiagnosed by my doctor, who prescribed medication for indigestion. From my medical history and symptoms, she should have made the link with my ovaries.

My doctor told me she would discuss the symptoms with a gynaecologist but when this didn't happen, I sought the Lord. It was so precise in what He showed me. In a dream, I saw a picture, of water pouring out of my stomach. The full understanding came when I visited the accident and emergency department for the second time.

The consultant used the exact words to describe the picture in my dream. "You have water on your belly, but I don't know how it got there," he told me. I was sent for a Computer Tomography scan (CT scan). It was Stage 3 ovarian cancer. I underwent extensive surgery, followed by chemotherapy treatment. I didn't have the focus to do any writing.

Frustrated, exhausted, and disillusioned with the many years of challenging a resource-led system that was discriminative, incompetent and characterised by a blame culture, I became physically and emotionally exhausted. Evidently, stress from the experience had contributed to the diagnoses. After writing many letters, which were dismissed, we made a formal complaint to senior managers of Social Care. Eventually, they upheld our complaints, but no one was held accountable for the mistakes and poor decisions that had been made. The mismanagement of our case would affect our children for the rest of their lives.

It was during the periods, before and after the diagnoses, that I felt the urge to include, in my book, the traumatic experience we had of the Social Care and the judicial systems. It started in 2004 and continued sporadically over the next twelve years.

The Oxford dictionary defines the word "journey" as '*a process of transition or progress; a long and often difficult process of personal change and development.*' (Dictionaries n.d.)

One of the hardest lessons in life is letting go of what we know, whether guilt, anger, love, loss or betrayal. We fight to hold on, and we fight to let go. Sometimes, change is not easy. This was the situation with me and my children. Although Tony had come to the decision long before me, I wasn't ready to let go, but continued fighting our corner for the sake of the children. I wasn't listening to my body and those who loved me. More importantly, I wasn't listening to what Father God had been saying for quite some time. Eventually, I elected to take my hands off the driver's wheel. I heard the Father say to me in a dream, *"Finally. I was waiting for you to do just that."*

In the dream, I recall seeing the presence of a man who I knew was Jesus. He was sitting down. I was standing up, but soon realised He wanted me to sit down in the seat next to Him. As I sat down, I remember feeling exhausted and laying my head on His shoulder. I knew then that it was time to commit the matter totally over to Him and rest in His Grace. He loved me and would take care of us. I found strength in this verse: *"Casting all your cares [all your anxieties, all your worries, and all your concerns, once and for all] on Him, for He cares about you [with deepest affection, and watches over you very carefully]"* (1 Peter 5:7). This was the impetus I needed to focus on what was really important to me—to enjoy my life and family.

The final push for writing came from a book I had read: *"Understanding Your Potential"*, by the late Myles Munroe. I was greatly challenged by the picture he painted of the stark reality that people carry the books, they should have written, within them to the grave. There is so much untapped potential in our graveyards. I was even more challenged when I officiated at the funeral of a fellow minister and friend. For many years she had spoken about writing her autobiography, but sadly, it didn't materialise before she died.

Writing my story has brought back painful memories from the past, but it has also given me inner healing and closure. It has helped me to move into the next season of my life.

In 2014 ovarian cancer returned. At the time, I had hoped to have launched my book. Since then, I've undergone further conventional and integrative treatments. Walking through this process, another time, has strengthened my relationships with my husband, Tony, and our families. Most of all, the relationship with my heavenly Father became an incredible and humbling experience.

Even though it feels like decades of struggles, the miracles along the way have far outweighed those challenges. Remarkably, they have been the springboard I've needed to begin sharing my story. C.S.

Lewis said: *"Hardship often prepares an ordinary person for an extraordinary destiny."* (C.S. Lewis).[1]

> "Hardship often prepares an ordinary person for an extraordinary destiny." —C.S. Lewis.

I hope my story will resonate with those who are facing similar health challenges. You too can overcome every obstacle and become extraordinary in the Kingdom of God.

## Part 2—Childhood

We are shaped by our core values and principles, cultural heritage and belief systems of our parents. Even our experience of the world, the influences of our environment, our peers and the choices we make, have all affected the person we become.

I'm fascinated by the 46 chromosomes we inherit from our parents—fathers being the major contributor to our DNA—and how they are distributed. But who decides which of the million of sperms will ultimately become a person? Yet, we were in the mind of God long before we were ever birthed in the earthly realm. Solomon, the writer of Ecclesiastes says, *'Just as you do not know the way and path of the wind or how the bones are formed in the womb of a pregnant woman, even so you do not know the activity of God who makes all things'* (Ecclesiastes 11:5).

My parents were married in 1949 in the West Indies. Their marriage brought seven children—four girls and three boys. My older sister, Eileen, and I are fourteen months apart. We were born in the West Indies and lived there until joining our parents in the UK. I'm the second child. I was born on a Monday. Yes, that old accentual nursery rhyme acclaimed to be written by Mother Goose. It says, *"Monday's child is fair of face."* Interestingly, 'fair of face' is said to be beautiful, auspicious and fortunate!

Jamaica was an English colony from 1655 and a British Colony from 1707, until its own independence in 1962. I was born seven years before this momentous event. I have very little recollection of my first six years there. I attended a private nursery in Trinity Ville, St. Thomas, where we lived. My father immigrated to England shortly after I was born, leaving us with our mother. Mum joined him later and we were left with different aunts. Eil (as she is affectionately known) and I were very close. The separation created a further blow to us as we didn't see each other until we travelled to England in 1961.

Memories of the time we spent apart are sparse, but my father's youngest sister, Aunt Vidal took care of me. She told me that whenever I saw an aeroplane, I pointed to the sky and said, "Mamma and papa up dey." I have a distinctive British accent and just can't imagine speaking Patois. My aunt was perhaps too young, to have had the responsibility of taking care of me. On the other hand, Aunt Sylvia, Mum's sister, who was much older, couldn't have looked after both of us. I was obviously upset, and wondered when I would see my mother again.

I remember the feeling of excitement at the prospect of being reunited with Eil. When I arrived, we were out playing together on the veranda, when my aunt shouted to my sister, "*Eileen, fetch me the chimmey pot!*" Attempting to please my aunt, I outraced my sister and ended up falling down and breaking my arm. I 'fibbed' on my sister and told my aunt that she had pushed me down on the veranda because I was fearful of getting into trouble. Fear has been a major challenge in my life. Eil received a good telling off but didn't say anything different. It was very grown up of her. I didn't own up that it was my own fault and arrived in the UK with my left arm in plaster.

My parents' decision to immigrate to England was not taken lightly. Their intention was to build a better life for the family. In June 1961, accompanied by a family friend, we arrived in Nottingham at the age of 6 and 7.

We found the UK a cold place and in stark contrast to the hot climate of the Caribbean. This was the first time I had seen my father. I don't remember feeling anxious about seeing him; neither do I recall there being any detrimental impact on me. Things just seemed to fall into place. As a child, I was very accepting. The nurture I received from my mother in my formative years, had somehow, bridged the gap. In time to come, I would learn how important it was to have a stable and secure family life in a child's formative years.

Separation can often be fraught with emotional turmoil for children. One of my friends shared the difficult experience he had of meeting his parents for the first time. It was "like meeting complete strangers," he told me. He recounted how, after making it to the airport by himself, he waited for his transport. A strange looking woman walked towards him. He was about 12 years' old. He remembered referring to her politely as "aunty" but was severely rebuked, and in no uncertain tone, she told him, "Pickney I'm yu madda!" which means, 'Child, I'm your mother!' The impact of separation can be grossly underestimated.

In those days it was common practice for parents to come to England without their children. The longer children lived with the extended family, the greater their attachment and the more distressing it was for them to leave behind familiar faces and the life they were accustomed to. Children experience trauma, loss, and separation because of the unfamiliar environment and culture into which they are thrown. This may well affect them into adulthood. Transition needs to be handled sensitively.

My parents were staunch Christians, and we were brought up with the same values. Family devotions were an important part of our lives. Every Sunday morning before we went to church, we were called into our parents' room for prayer. Usually, that would be around 6 o'clock in the morning when we were in deep sleep. It was a struggle to get up so early. We sang songs and read from the Bible.

One by one our names were called out to pray. Kneeling around the bed, you could hear the whisper of a few sentences which we copied from our parents. (I smile even now that I passed on the same values to my own children). Whenever my children, Jason and Jenny had disagreements, the prayer, might go something like this: ". . . and God, please help 'Jason' to keep his eyes closed when he is praying." Obviously, Jenny said this for our benefit, hoping that this would land Jason in trouble. The only way she could have known Jason's eyes were open was if hers were open, too!

My father was always the last person to pray, and when he did, we all fell asleep. Dad's prayers were very long and loud. We were convinced he'd wake up the entire neighbourhood and the thought of that made us cringe!

My mother, a woman of faith, love and prayer, was very astute. Her skills as a seamstress and baker were next to none. We have not met anyone who can compete with her. She followed recipes up to a point but had a sixth sense when it came to baking the best cake you have ever tasted. (I am of course biased). She was so creative that she even began writing her own recipes.

Mum's home-made cakes were often Christmas presents for people living on their own. The aroma of freshly baked cakes would fill the house. When she had finished preparing the cake mixture, Mum always left some in the bowl. She never needed to shout to let us know. Very quickly, a stampede of small feet emerged from wherever we were in the house, to devour the cake mix she had left for us to enjoy. I guess it was one of the only times we responded to Mum so quickly!

Mum had many strings to her bow. As a silver service waitress, we were used to 'fine dining,' and were taught table manners and etiquette. Our friends were always impressed by Mum's three-course meals. They loved coming over for dinner. Mum's cooking was nutritious and creative. The meals she produced were not typical of West Indian cuisine but were inspired by cuisines from around the world.

Once a month Mum gave us the dreaded 'washout' made up of bitter herbs. It was an unpleasant detox and needed 'just a spoon full of sugar to make the medicine go down,' to cleanse the system. It seemed to go down faster when we pinched our noses.

Mum spoke the Queen's English almost perfectly! When the house phone rang, she went from reprimanding us about something we did to her pleasant phone voice. She sounded delightful in her manner. We called it her 'telephone voice.' Mum would cross her legs and sit comfortably in the armchair in preparation for the long conversations she would sometimes have. In fact, I don't recall hearing my parents speaking Patois, except when they were annoyed with us. I learnt to speak Patois from my friends, and actually there is an art to it.

Mum passed on her dressmaking skills to her girls, but none of us can bake as well as her. She had strength, resilience, endurance, and epitomised Isaiah 30:15:

*. . . In quietness and in confidence shall be your strength.*

Mum worked tirelessly in various jobs as well as Dad's businesses. Dad taught her to drive and for a while, she worked as one of his taxi drivers. At that time she was one of a few Black female drivers in Nottingham. I can't ever imagine how Mum was able to do all of this, while bringing up the seven of us.

There were many funny moments, growing up. Among the funniest, were the numerous times when Mum just couldn't remember our names. She would do a roll call of all the names, while the person she wanted stood quietly in front of her, before getting to the right one. I can still remember the lovely way she chuckled to herself.

From a young age, Dad had been a provider for his siblings, which resulted in him spending very little time in education. Consequently, there was a strong emphasis placed on our education. Very often we were reminded that 'education and manners will take you around the world.' I remember times when Dad would arrive home and, randomly, test us on our timetables. Mum and Dad had high expectations of us and did not compromise when it came to our education. They encouraged us to optimise the opportunities they didn't have, but not in the sense of trying to live their lives through us. My Father, at one time, bought an entire library of encyclopaedia books, expecting us to read them all.

As the older children, my sister and I were tasked with teaching our younger siblings to read and write long before they started school. This is a practice of most Black families where education is valued. There was little time for play; most of the time was spent with our heads in our books, doing chores, and working in my father's businesses without pay! In today's terms, this would be viewed as child labour.

Dad's entrepreneurship began after an accident at work, where he sustained severe burns to his face and body. This frightened me and it took me a while to visit him in the hospital. A family friend had taken me to see him. I was afraid that he would look different. Apparently, I was so shocked when I saw him; I ended up eating a banana, complete with its skin! Dad went away to convalesce and made a full physical recovery, much to the surprise of the doctors.

Dad never spoke about the emotional impact it had on him but after he recovered, he vowed never to work for anyone again and started his own business. At that time he was a driving instructor and owned a driving school, which he proudly called, 'Friendly School of Motoring.' Dad worked arduously around the clock to provide for his family.

After some years, he bought a grocery shop, which was within walking distance of our home. Finally, he started his own taxi rank and purchased a fleet of cars. He had a sixth sense when it came to his cars. Many people have witnessed my father falling asleep at the wheel of his car as it waited at the traffic lights. Somehow he knew when the traffic lights turned to green. People watched with their mouths open as he drove the car away at the right time, even though it appeared Dad was still asleep. I am still intrigued by how he did this.

Dad was a great business pioneer for the Black and Asian communities. There have been numerous people from these communities who have commended Dad for his generousity and kindness in providing employment for them and helping their families.

In the 1960's and 1970's entrepreneurship was a remarkable achievement in our community. Dad was ambitious and challenged the status quo!

Dad was affectionate but he was a disciplinarian. When he left for work, he told Mum to record everything we did wrong, and on his return home he would address any issues! That was putting it mildly, as we would be physically chastised. When we misbehaved, and no one owned up, we were given an ultimatum that everyone would get into trouble that day. On several occasions, we were saved just in time! Whenever Dad looked in my direction, I was so fearful that I would start crying. He knew that my fear of chastisement meant I was more likely to behave and he would often say, "I wouldn't even put a finger on you." I found out that that technique worked in my favour, so I grew up hardly ever putting a foot wrong with Dad. My response to Mum was very different. I was well known for answering her back. Mum would chase after me but could never catch me as I was a lot faster than she was.

I recall the times when I felt the security of having a father at home. Dad worked night shifts. There were times I couldn't sleep until I knew he was home. I listened out to hear the key turning in the front door and the door quietly closing. Immediately I fell asleep. Dad was home.

Dad's presence gave me a sense of security. I have never felt as secure driving with anyone else as I did with my father. An important lesson I learnt in life, was the importance of having the security of a father in my life.

I pause to reflect on the occasion when my parents took all six of us to buy new shoes. My youngest sister wasn't born at the time. It was like a family day out for us. We were invited to a wedding and were all going. Fascinated at how well-mannered we were, the shop assistant was eager to please and made a huge fuss over us. That day we each had a new pair of white shoes.

Dad was a proud man. In our teenage years, there were times when we wanted to go to a church convention, but weren't allowed to go unless we had new clothes to wear. I shed many tears when we couldn't get to go. Even after pleading with him, he wouldn't change his mind. When one of the adults made a plea on our behalf, Dad still wouldn't budge, and Mum seemed to support his decision.

I'm saddened about the period when Mum was left to bring us up alone. For most of our adolescence, Dad was an absent father. The boys, in particular, were affected by the lack of affirmation they received from him. All they wanted was his approval and to hear him say how proud he was of them. I have great admiration and respect for my mother. She has always been our bedrock. After Dad died, she kept us all together. Her home was the central point for all of the gatherings with her children and grandchildren. Having said this, I have always held both my parents in high esteem and appreciate the sacrifices they made for me.

## Part 3—Adolescence

When my parents arrived in England, like so many other families from the Caribbean, they did not intend to stay for more than a few years. But for many reasons, beyond their control, they spent the rest of their lives here.

During the war, thousands of Caribbean men and women were recruited and served in the armed forces, where they made enormous contributions to the freedom of this country. When the war ended in 1945, the government recognised that the country needed more labour:

*Immigration from the West Indies was encouraged by the British Nationality Act of 1948, which gave all Commonwealth citizens entry into Britain* (Archives n.d.).

Economic opportunities were the primary factor for many families coming from the Caribbean to the UK. Most of those who settled in Britain in the mid to late 20th century came after 1948 when the *Empire Windrush*, and other ships, brought people from the West Indies to help with the post-war reconstruction of the UK.

At the time overt racism was rife. During the first three years or so, my parents rented rooms, which was the norm for most migrants. In certain areas, they were not welcomed by the indigenous people. I don't recall hearing them discussing their feelings about their experiences. However, many individuals from my parents' generation endured the derogatory notices that landlords displayed in the windows. '*No Blacks, No Irish and No dogs here.*' And yet my parents worked very hard for what they had, and they were resilient. Our heavenly Father was always faithful in His provision.

My parents purchased their property, a large family house, which one of our cousins described as "very grand with high ceilings." It had a lot of character and featured a large hand painted mural on the wall of the stairwell. I often wonder how valuable that painting would be today. I spent the next 20 years living in the family home and certainly have many happy and challenging memories of the time spent there.

We were one of the first Black families to live in that neighbourhood. I remember how excited we were as children when we were having the back garden pebbled. The black tarmac looked impressive against the white specks in between. The large gate that led to the back yard separated us from the old lady living next door. At the side of her house was a large workshop full of paints and equipment.

The owners kept a large wheelbarrow on one side, and nails were sticking out of it. Our parents warned us of the danger, but we saw it as a great place of adventure and got up to many tricks. There was an occasion when we were all playing on the wheelbarrow and my sister, Rose, slipped and caught her leg on one of the nails. We watched as blood poured from her leg! She ended up with a telling off from Dad before being taken to the hospital. I guess he was cross and frightened, at the same time, by the prospect of what could have been.

Having passed my Eleven-plus, I was ready to face whatever lay ahead, on the horizon, at senior school. Emotionally, I was afraid of the unknown but judging from my outward appearance, no one would ever know how I felt inside. Smartly dressed in my new uniform—blouse, tie, pleated skirt and shoes, I left for school. When I returned home, I looked the exact opposite of that.

My skirt was almost down to my ankles, hair in a mess and my shoes were scuffed! All in one day! My older sister was quite the opposite of me. She didn't have a single hair out of place, yet she got involved in fights: many of them in my defence! If anyone wanted a fight, I only had to say "I'm going to get my BIG sister." Bless her, she wasn't much bigger than me, but she stood for no nonsense with the 'White kids.' She was escorted home almost every day by her admirers—boys.

The year before I passed my Eleven-plus, the education system had been restructured. This meant I would attend the Ellis Guilford Bilateral School, which was a school in our catchment area. A bilateral school contains both grammar and non-selective streams where the two groups of students attended together. I was put in the grammar stream and chose the commercial course. It wasn't hard to decide on what I wanted to be—I just followed Eil. It was the era where we sat at single desks, with the inkwells and fountain pens.

As a Black student, there wasn't the variety of choices available to us, no matter how clever we were. The British Education system allowed me to at least achieve some CSE qualifications, but it was during a year's course in college that I really excelled. It was here that I gained more qualifications in commercial studies. I was now a 17-year-old, with short hair, and a spotty face. I was shy and lacking in confidence because of my self-image. I enjoyed the year at college more than I did senior school. By the time I had finished that year, my confidence was ignited, and I became more assertive.

At home, we didn't do any of the girly things like experimenting with makeup, nail varnish and jewellery. At that time those were some of the things forbidden by the church. Despite the fact that my parents were married with rings, the church introduced a ruling where members were not allowed to wear jewellery, including wedding rings! Nevertheless, we knew where Mum had kept her ring. When she wasn't at home, we would climb on chairs to get to the top shelf of her wardrobe, where we found it. We dressed in her clothes and paraded about in her ring. I don't recall where Dad kept his.

The stockings I wore, in my teenage years, were held up by suspenders. They were always too big for my skinny legs. There were many times when Dad would see me and say, 'You never look good yet!' His remarks were unhelpful, to say the least, but I'm sure he didn't mean any harm. However, his words were sharp and contributed to my low self-esteem. In time to come, I learnt just how much impact words can have on your self-esteem and how impressionable children are. Adolescence is a time when we need our father's approval.

There is a tendency to remember the happier times in our lives and suppress memories that are painful and uncomfortable. My childhood memories were the happiest.

The challenges of overt racism in the 1960's onwards affected my teenage years but somehow I developed the skills to survive. In the 21st century, racism is more institutionalised.

At school, there was a lot of name-calling, but we were tough kids in our makeup, and this made us more determined to strive to be better than our White counterparts. *"When something bad happens you have three choices. You can let it define you, let it destroy you, or you can let it strengthen you"* (Unknown author).[2]

"When something bad happens, you have three choices. You can let it define you, let it destroy you, or you can let it strengthen you" —Unknown author

I learnt quickly that we had to work twice as hard in order to achieve our career goals and make something of our lives.

The teachers were unsympathetic and very little was done to alleviate the problem. This was a time when the teacher's word was upheld by the school. My parents, especially my father, would take the teacher's word as gospel. In the Caribbean, it was the same practice. If word got home that something happened in school, children would be reprimanded for the second time. For this reason, we avoided telling our parents. At any rate, I rarely got into trouble at school, and in my 5th Year, I was elected a school prefect, a title that wasn't given lightly. The younger students looked up to us as role models. It was an era where the headmaster used the slipper and cane as physical punishment. We were disciplined for the occasional answering back or lack of concentration in our classes. I was a regular recipient of white chalk being thrown at my forehead by the geography teacher.

While I was never caned at school, I witnessed one of my friends being caned in the palm of her hand. She turned into two different colours—red and then grey. I thought she was going to pass out, but she was very brave. Later, I asked, "Did it hurt?" And of course it did, but it was a matter of maintaining her dignity. Crying in front of her peers would be more of an embarrassment.

I experienced the wrath of a teacher who actually punched me for breaking a school rule—walking on the grass! My friend and I had used the grass area as a shortcut. The teacher was heavily built, a short male Caucasian, who was named quite appropriately as Mr. Lyon. He called us both over and threw a punch at the side of my face with his huge fist. I suffered a hard blow to my face which almost knocked me out. I still remember telling myself 'I mustn't faint. Just don't faint'. The impact of that blow affected me in years to come. A large lump grew on the same side of my face. Eventually, the lump was removed. It turned out to be a parotid tumour. Parotid tumours are abnormal growths within the glands which are mostly benign (non-cancerous). Mine was benign. Ten years later it grew back, and I went through another operation.

For many years, I didn't disclose the incident to anyone. I felt embarrassed and responsible that it was my own fault. I was fearful that there would be some kind of repercussion, and that the teachers wouldn't believe me.

Had it happened today, Mr. Lyons would certainly have been charged with assault and it was highly probable that he would have been dismissed from teaching. I kept this secret for many years, and it was only after leaving school that I disclosed it to my parents. They were shocked, horrified and angry all at the same time, and could not understand why I hadn't told them before. By this time, Dad was less strict than I remember from my younger days.

Years later, it didn't even occur to me that I could have taken action against the teacher. I had moved on but later I learnt Mr. Lyon collapsed and died in school. I should have spoken up at that time. He had breached his trust and care towards his students. It should never have happened. I certainly didn't deserve such cruelty.

Maths was not my favourite subject. In fact, my Maths teacher wrote in my school report that he believed I would '*need a good horoscope to help me to pass the exam on the day!*' I ended up with a minus somewhere in the results! It was a self-fulfilling prophecy, and for many years, I struggled with Maths. I felt inadequate and afraid to ask for help in front of others for fear of being ridiculed. So here I was going through adolescence, lacking in confidence, and at times feeling very insecure and depressed and wanting to run away!

## Part 4—Adulthood

My 18th birthday was a pivotal moment of development when the 'duckling turned into a beautiful swan.' I was even interested in boys and went through the physiological and emotional aspects of adolescence. My children make fun of me when I remind them that it wasn't that long ago that I was their age, "But that was back in the day Mum!" they would say.

Maxi dresses were in fashion in the 1970's, and it was the time when we made most of our clothes. I made one for my birthday party. It was a fitted A-line dress with short sleeves. I wore a chiffon scarf and an impressive broach on it. Mum was always on hand to help us whenever we got stuck with the pattern. Mum baked a cake as she always did.

When I finished college, I applied for my first job and got it. I worked as a personal assistant to one of the partners in a chartered accountancy firm. It was no coincidence that the company was located on 'Wheeler' Gate. Eil worked at Barclays Bank, one of the Big Four banks just around the corner from me. We often met up for lunch.

Our monthly salary contributed to running the family home. I didn't appreciate it at the time, but the experience gave me a sense of responsibility and helped me develop character. Even in tough financial times, we prospered.

It was an exciting period for me. But who would have thought it possible that I ended up working with figures after that negative comment from my Maths teacher? At last, that self-fulfilling prophecy was broken. After 5 years, in 1978, I left that company.

Throughout my working career, I've never experienced unemployment. I firmly believe this was due to the good work ethics I inherited from my parents.

My NHS career began in 1979, at the Family Practitioner Committee. I was a personal assistant to the assistant administrator and the finance officer.

I attribute all my successes to Father God. I moved locations and worked my way up the ladder and into management roles. This culminated in my giving 35 years of service to the NHS.

After I retired from the NHS, the idea of setting up my own business was a natural progression. I had no intention of calling it a day. One opportunity had led to another. My teaching and leadership qualifications had also equipped me to complete a business course. I was well positioned to launch a new business.

I reflect on my values and principles of faith; the security and nurturing of my formative years; the positives and negatives of church life; my cultural heritage, the circles of influence and the challenges of life. They have all shaped me into the person I am.

There was a period in my life when Mum and my youngest sibling, Marina lived with her sister, Aunt Sylvia and husband, Uncle Oscar in America. By then I was in my early twenties and was 'parent' to my three youngest siblings. During this time I had a horrible fire accident at home. We were going to a youth convention in Leeds in the church van (minibus). My brothers got ready while I prepared breakfast. I was cooking fried dumpling when it happened. Somehow water dropped into the hot Dutch pot and set the pot on fire. I remember an explosion and heat penetrating my skin. I sustained burns to my face, neck and chest. My brothers ran up the road to my father's grocery shop. He arrived within minutes, and drove me to the hospital. They told us they didn't have the facility to treat me, so Dad had to take me to the accident and emergency at the new hospital several miles away. I screamed all the way there.

Mum and Marina were still in America. I was transferred to the eye hospital and spent several weeks there. The doctors were afraid I would lose my eyesight and be scarred for life. After my discharge, one of the women in the church, Mother Davy, offered to take care of me. Even though she had a large family, I had my own room and convalesced at her home for a while. I have always been thankful for her act of kindness. Although I fully recovered I was left traumatised by the experience. Because of my accident, Mum and Marina returned home sooner than scheduled.

Years later, I can still remember hearing the conversation Mum was having with my sister: "Eileen, I can't believe it, Hyacinth's changed. Tony has swept her off her feet!" she giggled. Mum was so happy at the prospect that true love was in the air. At the time of their conversation, I had reached a quarter of a century. Eil was married and lived in Bristol. I was still at home with three of my siblings.

In 1981 Tony and I met in Bible School; it was love at first sight. We received various confirmations that we were meant for each other. For example, when I was out shopping with Mum one day, we saw Tony driving by at the precise moment. Talk about the right timing. When he blew his horn, I pretended I didn't see him. It wasn't a matter of playing 'hard to get,' I was quite shy.

My social life revolved around church, and I am the first to admit that 'church,' as well as my upbringing, were overly protective towards the young people at that time. I was naïve, and lived a sheltered life. In contrast, Tony was a man of the world. As a new Christian, he attended the Mansfield Church of God of Prophecy where he lived. Our relationship blossomed from there on.

We courted for six months, and Tony asked Mum for my hand in marriage. I honestly thought she was not going to agree. We invited him over for dinner to meet the family, and Mum cross-examined him. As we sat eating together at the dining table, Tony felt so nervous that he almost poured out the entire bottle of salad cream over his meal. We were all stunned into silence for a good five minutes. My sister, Marina was about 6 years' old at the time. Her laughter broke the silence and we all joined in.

Being the gentleman he was, Tony proposed to me, on one knee. Mum was incredible in taking on the role of both parents. I passed my driving test in the October, which was a lovely engagement present, and we celebrated our engagement with our parents, the pastor and his wife.

A year later, I married my 'knight in shining armour,' and he carried me over the threshold to our new life together. That day, I felt like a princess. Dad drove me to church in his white Mercedes Benz and proudly walked me up the aisle. We had 350 guests and counting. Although we planned the wedding, we were supported by our parents, family, and friends.

Tony owned his house, and after we were married, I moved in with a few 'bottom draw' items. Gradually, I added a few feminine touches to our home. Refurbishing the property was great fun because we had similar taste in furnishings. I commuted to work in Nottingham for a while until I got a job nearer home.

The new role was working at the pathology laboratory. I worked as part of the blood bank and immunology staff. We wore white coats, and the team were regularly mistaken for doctors. I was the only person of colour in the whole of the department.

I can remember a particular day when a young child, attending the clinic with her grandmother, shouted, "Look Grandma!" The waiting area was full of patients that day. It appeared as if the child had not seen a Black person before, and I must admit there weren't many Black families in the area. She pointed her finger towards me and followed me until I was out of sight. Everyone stared at me. I felt my colour rising up with embarrassment. I gave her a little wave and said, "Hello." Turning to the child, the grandmother said, "Yes it's that lovely lady!"

From 1983 to 2002, I had a succession of jobs at the hospital. I worked in the paediatric assessment unit, mental health unit and patient administration services. By 2007 the acute hospitals around the country had changed to foundational trusts. Trust hospitals had to demonstrate their commitment to delivering quality services to patients on a sustainable basis, and have a degree of independence from the Department of Health.

Having moved to the Nottingham University Trust Hospital, I worked in the adult services of Health and Social Care, where I managed staff, resources and systems across the different campuses. Finally, I ended up teaching in Learning and Organisational Development.

I realised that the further I moved up the ladder, the more I was in the minority. There were a lot of inequalities in the system and fewer opportunities for minority groups. However, my love for people grew stronger, and I excelled in those challenging times. One thing led to another and I moved into different arenas. I created education curricula for corporate training and lecturing. I took every opportunity given to me for public speaking.

Like most public service providers, organisational changes are inevitable. The NHS is no different. It is a vast and complex organisation that is impacted on many levels. The government is the main driving force of change. Their main objective is to bring continuous improvement to the quality of healthcare provision. Also, the NHS has to adapt to new policies and legislation that are introduced by new governments.

I've seen numerous changes during my NHS career. Some have worked and others haven't. At the time I managed large staff groups, there were over 100 team members. I recruited, appraised and trained staff. An important part of my task was to analyse the impact of change on the staff, the resources and the systems. Equally important, my leadership qualities enabled me to manage the resistance and barriers to change through to the implementation stage. The medical consultant staff was the main driving force but, at the same time, the most difficult group of people to bring on board. The consultants were very 'old school' in their views, and were from the era where the junior doctors walked behind them: a practice that is still in existence (junior doctors as entourage).

As I continued to grow in confidence and assertiveness, the challenges helped to refine my character. Even though I flourished in the working environment, it was the grace of God that sustained me in weathering the storms.

For twelve years I managed the largest staff group at King's Mill Hospital, NHS Trust. My White colleagues, appointed after me, were mentored by me, but quickly promoted, while I remained on the same grade. Ironically, close to the time of my departure from the NHS, I ran the mentoring scheme for senior managers in a different NHS Trust. I've noticed all along how Father God uses negative situations and turns them around for my good and the good of others.

To varying degrees, the NHS is still institutionally racist. Only a small percentage of minority staff is promoted to executive levels of the organisation. We still face the same challenges, but they are packaged in a different way. I've had first-hand experience of supporting minority people who literally have been hounded out of their careers because of the colour of their skin. This continues to happen in both the private and public sectors. I believe the decision, to leave the NHS, was made at the right time.

At my leaving party, I was intrigued by a card given to me by one of my staff. It said something like: 'It doesn't matter where you go, so long as you're going in the right direction.' The words resonated with me. In time, it would become instrumental in creating a name for my business.

I discovered how fulfilled I was when I was teaching, interacting with people and helping others. Teaching became my vocation, purpose, and calling. With the help of my brother, Peter, I chose the name 'Alignment with Purpose Consultancy.' My slogan is 'to empower people to find their purpose and destiny, and make a living from what they enjoy doing.' The lesson in life is: "Don't waste another day just existing and disliking what you do."

> "Don't waste another day just existing and disliking what you do."

Years later, my husband went for a private orthopaedic consultation. It transpired that the consultant, his wife and I had all worked together. When he realised that Tony was my husband, he told him: 'Hyacinth practically ran King's Mill hospital!'

We spent our married lives on the move and worked in full-time jobs. We travelled from one end of the country to the other to attend church events. I prepared sermons for preaching and teaching and delivered training and workshops. At the time, I was the leader of the *One Accord* Gospel Group, and we were performing in different parts of the country. Even on weekends, we were entertaining family and friends. We were accustomed to a fast pace of life.

As a qualified motor mechanic, Tony spent a great deal of his spare time repairing vehicles for family and friends. He worked in the mining industry, and this left very little time for us. But the time came when we travelled across the UK, Europe, USA, Canada and the Caribbean.

We moved from our matrimonial home after 10 years. Tony had been commuting to Nottingham for work. After finishing work one day, he felt the Lord leading him to what would become our home for the next 25 years. Our house was sold after the third viewing. Mum and Eil came to see our new house and agreed it was the right one. We looked forward to the move but were disappointed when the estate agency selling the property called to tell us the sale would no longer go ahead. The vendors had a change of heart, and the property was taken off the market.

Distraught by the news, we rented a house from a friend. I wasn't in the least bit interested in any other property and didn't want to buy for the sake of having somewhere to live. Father God knows the desire of our hearts. Sometime after this, we received another call. "Mrs. Fraser, the house that you really like, is back on the market; the vendors have had a change in their circumstances." We welcomed the news, and in 1991 we moved to our new home.

When Mum was alive, I had successfully gained a new management position nearer home. She knew I was going for the interview. "You'll get the job with ease," she said, and of course I did. Mum spoke uplifting words. By this point, I knew the Lord was strategically positioning me for my next transition.

The new job was a stepping stone to fulfilling the call I had on my life for teaching. I decided to take a month's break before I started the new job. It would be the first time in the whole of my career, or at least that was what I had hoped for. Contrary to this, Tony decided it was a good opportunity to introduce me to a new puppy he had always wanted—a Dalmatian.

He had left several clues around the house, and even when I heard him talking to someone on the subject of dogs, the penny hadn't dropped. While Tony drove Eil and me to my leaving party, we were having a conversation. Eil had mentioned how much I was looking forward to the break. That's when Tony made the revelation, and the next thing we knew was when he announced that the dog would be arriving the following day! Zak was just a few weeks old and very cute. I ended up spending the entire month helping with the new puppy. I really didn't mind as he was so adorable.

# STEP 1—DISCOVERY OF SELF

## An awakening of God

Growing up, my whole world revolved around 'Church' and I knew nothing else. In any event, I had no options. Even if I didn't want to go, I went because I wasn't a rebellious child. My parents were good role models. They were born again Christians and members of a Pentecostal church, the Church of God of Prophecy. Born again is to surrender your life to Christ, asking Him into your heart and making Him Lord and Saviour.

> *For with the heart a person believes [in Christ as Saviour] resulting in his justification [that is, being made righteous—being freed of the guilt of sin and made acceptable to God]; and with the mouth he acknowledges and confesses [his faith openly], resulting in and confirming [his] salvation* (Romans 10:10).

In the early 1950's, Pentecostalism was brought to these shores from the Caribbean countries by our parents' generation. Churches started out as house groups and later moved to rented halls, before acquiring their own buildings.

I came from a very talented family—music, art, and design were among our gifts. As young as 3 and 4 years old, my sister and I were on stage reciting the books of the Bible in front of large congregations. We had to stand on chairs so that we could be seen. Eil read music and played the piano as we sang together.

I first discovered my love and natural talent for playing the piano. Eil was dedicated to practising and tried to teach me to read music, but I found it difficult and soon we abandoned the idea. Whenever I heard her practising at home, I realised I could play note by note from memory. Although I can play the keyboard without practising, reading music is one of my life's goals.

Growing up, we started a group called the *Wheelers Six*. We practised regularly and performed at church events, using our own materials. My brothers and youngest sister are talented and creative in music and art. Each of them has had their own bands, and travelled across the globe performing. At the same time, my sister Rosemarie was very fashion conscious and excelled as a stunning professional model. My brother Sam was also a successful model, and this took him across Europe.

When they were young, Sam and Clement taught themselves to play instruments. They made drums out of tins and cardboard boxes. They also used their voices as music, and the sounds were incredible—today it's called beat boxing. Peter learnt to play the guitar, and his first guitar was a ukulele. I also recall the times when Dad played the saxophone well.

In our teenage years, Eil was the first leader of the gospel group, the *One Accord*. We had a unique harmony. The group was comprised mainly of family and friends from church. It took us across the UK performing at national and local events, on the radio and in recording studios. Regrettably, while we were known for our harmonies, we didn't get around to making a record. *One Accord* became a significant part of my life.

Gospel music has its roots in enslavement, and many songs were borne out of those struggles. Successful artists such as Whitney Houston, Aretha Franklin, Stevie Wonder, Lionel Ritchie, Michael Jackson and many others began their singing career in the church.

The successes we had were pivotal to our early years in the church, and this led the way for many young people to discover their talents, gifts, and career paths.

As a disciplined person, I usually consider the consequences of my actions before stepping out to do anything. In my early teens, I felt I had had enough of house chores and decided to run away from home. When I got as far as the front door, I thought about what I would do to survive. I had no idea of where I would go and made the decision that it wasn't a good idea after all.

Long before I became a member of the Church of God of Prophecy, I followed its strict regime. I recall the time when the church held the view that it was an exclusive body of believers. This view wasn't unique to our church organisation as other churches held similar views.

We received the 'right hand of fellowship' to become members of the church. It involved agreeing to its *29 Prominent Bible Teachings* and its *Advice to Members*.

We held the Bible in our left hand and held up our right hand promising to accept the Bible as the Word of God, rightly divided; the New Testament as our rule of faith, doctrine and government and to walk in the light as it was revealed to us.

The time came when the Church of God of Prophecy had a paradigm shift, which changed our thinking about exclusiveness. Bishop Oswald Williams, the national overseer at the time, was instrumental in bringing about the vision of 'No More Strangers.' He led the way for the church to embrace other Christians as members of the wider body of Christ. It was unfortunate that Oswald's vision wasn't fully implemented before his appointment at the church's international offices in Cleveland Tennessee, USA.

Going to night clubs was against the *Advice to Members*. The rationale behind it was that new Christians would be led astray. The nearest I got to one was at the school disco! Had I mentioned the word 'disco' to my parents, they most certainly wouldn't have allowed me to go. I was determined to go to my end of Year 5 disco and led my parents to believe something else. I had sneaked a change of clothing with me.

At school, I was my own person and didn't give in to peer-pressure. My friends nicknamed me 'Christian' because I didn't do what they did. They teased me and said I couldn't dance and of course, it was simply not the case. I had to show them that I had rhythm and soon they found out for themselves.

My first experience of God was quite daunting. I was in no doubt that God was real. The church had rented a room at the Albert Hall on Friday evenings. There were a lot of young people in our church. Etega Wright was our pastor at the time. We were supposed to be on our knees praying, but I had fallen asleep.

Suddenly I heard a blast of trumpets playing—it was deafening! When I opened my eyes and looked around it was evident that no one else heard the music, as they continued praying. The sound became louder and louder. I was half expecting to see Jesus bursting through the clouds. My heart raced. A cold sweat came over me, and I thought that judgement day had arrived. It all seemed so real. I questioned whether I was ready to meet God. I was so relieved to find out that it wasn't a reality. Shortly after this experience, I gave my life to God. At the age of 16, I was baptised along with other members of the *One Accord*. We sang together, 'I'm gonna lay down my burden, down by the riverside.'

The occasion was one of many highlights that marked our reception into membership of the church. We had great admiration for Sister Wright, our pastor. Her home at Hood Street became our second home. We looked up to her, and she became a great influence in my life. I received the baptism of the Holy Spirit and spoke in other tongues at her home. Before she became our pastor, Etega was a National Youth Secretary of our church in the UK. She was a great visionary, who started the first youth convention held in our region at the church in Leeds.

My sister Eil and her husband Verley were youth camp directors for many years. We experienced the power of God in our lives. Youth conventions, youth and junior camps were instrumental in leading the young people to Christ. Many marriages came about as a result of these events.

Even though I was born again, from time to time my life would be filled with fear. It wasn't the reverential fear of God but the fear of the things I had no control over. From a child, I was afraid of the dark and sensed the evil around me. For many years fear controlled my life: fear of the unknown. I battled with negative thoughts and feelings.

Close to my 50th birthday came the start of serious health issues. By then I had lost the most significant people in my life—both of my parents. I found myself expecting things to go wrong, and that became an open door for attacks from the enemy—Satan. Soon, I accepted the fact that I needed a revelation of the Father's love.

I spent most of my life breaking free from a legalistic view of Christianity. I wanted to find God and not just attend religious activities. Wrong beliefs lead to wrong thinking. The Law of Moses teaches that no one can be good enough. Even if we broke one of the laws, we would be guilty of them all (James 2:12). I found out that Grace is a person—Jesus. Everything I needed was already in Him, ready for me to receive, by grace, through faith in the redemptive work of the cross. God desires His children to receive all He has provided. In the Greek, salvation means welfare, prosperity, healing, deliverance, preservation, and safety. I came to the conclusion I no longer needed to strive for forgiveness and the unconditional love of God. I needed to experience more of the Good news.

As the journey began to unfold, I wanted to understand what belonged to me. Christian TV provided opportunities to learn about Kingdom principles. It was exhilarating to hear Gloria Copeland say that God gave us 'Righteousness for our spirit man, peace for our minds and healing for our bodies.'

Although I had citizenship in the Kingdom of God, I knew very little of what belonged to me. I listened to Bible teachings from Bill Winston and learned that the Kingdom was a spiritual realm and he taught me how I should function in it. The way we receive spiritual blessings and promises is by speaking faith-filled words. The more I listened to the Word the more my faith grew (Romans 10:17). I learnt a lot from Eil and different teachers of the Kingdom. In particular, Andrew Wommack's CDs helped me to understand my authority as a believer. I started to call "Those things which are not, as though they were" (Romans 4:17) over my health.

Jesus had borne my sicknesses and carried my grief and pain. It meant that 'my cancer' was put on His body for me over 2,000 years ago. He took away this disease for me to the cross and conquered every sickness and disease—past, present and future.

The Word became my medicine, and I used it regularly. There are no negative side effects from the Word of God. Neither can you overdose on it. We stop the Word from working for us by our words: *"Death and life are in the power of the tongue, and those who love it and indulge it will eat its fruit and bear the consequences of their words"* (Proverbs 18:21).

I was overwhelmed by the power of God's love for me and renewed my mind to this truth. I no longer needed to strive to achieve, to impress or to be intimidated by others. Fear wasn't from the Father. '*For God did not give us a spirit of timidity or cowardice or fear, but He has given us a spirit of power and of love and of sound judgment and personal discipline*' (2 Timothy 1:17). Sickness wasn't from God, and He certainly doesn't use it to teach us a lesson. IT IS His will for His children to be healed and made whole. He is Jehovah Rapha—my healer, and Jehovah Jireh—my provider. He provides everything we need according to life and godliness. I didn't have to make it happen. That was my Father's responsibility. I was responsible to renew my mind to this truth. Learning to let go of wrong beliefs is a daily process.

## Walk in your purpose

Back in the 1970s, I first served as a Sunday School teacher. My pastor, Etega Wright, had given me a prophetic word. "Hyacinth," she said, "you're a born teacher!" but I couldn't see it myself, and had no idea at the time that it would be my vocation.

Later, however, I discovered a love and passion for teaching and compassion for others. My love for people came from a strong sense of injustice for people who were made to feel inferior or had been disadvantaged. I get a lot of enjoyment from serving others.

Browsing through the stationery store is one of my favourite past times. I get a buzz from looking at brightly coloured post-its, paper clips, pens, pencils, paper, card, etc. They are all part of the stock of teaching and learning materials I keep for my students and delegates.

Visualisation is my prominent learning style. Images, pictures and illustrations come very naturally to me. A Chinese Proverb says '*Tell me, I'll forget. Show me, I may remember, but involve me, and I'll understand.*'

> 'Tell me, I'll forget. Show me, I may remember, but involve me, and I'll understand.' —Chinese Proverb

I like to use different visual aids to support my learners and motivate them to put into practice what they have learned.

Getting involved in new projects is a great motivator for me. I consider it as an opportunity for personal development. I am committed to doing whatever it takes to deliver excellence, even though it sometimes pushes me to the limit.

Studying in higher education didn't come easy, as I had to work hard to achieve my goals. At the time I had my first management post, I was able to get on a management course. Although I failed the exam, I had top marks for my presentation skills work.

Many years later, I was completing a Post Graduate Certificate in Education (teacher's qualification), when I was given the news of breast cancer. I was overly stretched physically, and mentally, but I carried on like a martyr, without accepting my limitations. My tutor gave me an extension to complete the work, but it turned out that I was one of the first to hand it in.

My children nominated me as 'Superwoman.' They were 8 and 9, and for my birthday they bought a musical card with a picture of the TV star 'Superwoman.' Every time I opened the card, and it played the music theme, I would laugh. It was very insightful of them, but I continued to ignore the Father's promptings.

I headed up management and leadership teams; contributed to and wrote educational curricula, teaching and training packages, policies and procedures. I invigilated exams and lectured in higher education and enjoyed participating in public speaking.

Parallel to this work, I served in local, regional and national leadership positions of the church such as small groups, youth, women and children's ministries. I was appointed National Sunday School secretary by Bishop Oswald Williams, the national overseer at that time. I recruited a team from Regions 4 and 5 to work with me delivering courses on a rolling programme up and down the country. The members of my team were from professional backgrounds.

We travelled the country to most of the churches, equipping Sunday School teachers. Upon successful completion, students received a certified teacher's qualification. During the time I served as National Sunday School secretary, church membership in the UK had rapidly increased and grew beyond a 5,000 membership in over 100 congregations. The Church of God of Prophecy had become one of the largest and fastest growing Black led churches in the 1970s.

Having gone through the ministerial process, I became a licensed minister. In 1995, I was appointed pastor of the church in Mansfield by Bishop Les Graham, the national overseer. During the time I served as pastor, I helped to set up a project from scratch, which later became a charitable organisation and I served as chairperson and director.

I am the sort of person who doesn't like to let people down. On my curriculum vitae, I describe myself as *'Hard working, loyal, committed, dedicated, reliable, and meticulous.'* The adage, *'If you want something done, ask a busy person,'* is true but being too busy contributed to my ill health.

In recent years, I completed further qualifications up to a master's degree in Strategic Management and Leadership. My 'Claim to Fame' moment arrived at the time when the college, North Nottinghamshire, had used my graduation photographs in their prospectus to promote their Part-Time Courses for 2013-2014. It was ironic that the title of 'consultant' was written under my photograph and name, long before the idea of a business consultancy was ever conceived.

The college had used the phrase *Picture yourself here* to extensively advertise their message across the Bassetlaw District of Nottinghamshire.

My photographs and those of fellow students were placed on the college's website and on billboards, posters, postcards, bus shelters and in the Retford Times.

Little did I know, at that time, I would be invited back to the college a year later to be guest speaker at their higher award ceremony.

From left to right: Senior lecturer at Sheffield Hallam University, me and the principal of North Nottinghamshire College. This photograph was taken at the Higher Education Award Ceremony at their end of year graduation, 12th November 2013.

## Write down your goals

Writing your goals down gives a sense of clarity and permanence. Goals are designed to help us identify where we are and where we want to be. Using SMART objectives is a tool that does just that. The acronym stands for Specific, Measurable, Achievable, Realistic and Time-framed.

Putting first things first is another useful tool. It helps to identify the important and urgent against the non-important and non-urgent tasks. Prioritisation helped me alleviate the stress and strain of the day and keep calm. So, what's the secret?

Our lives are filled with 'busyness and distractions' leaving little room for the urgent and important things such as spending quality time in our relationships.

Starting the day with God through personal time talking to

Him, reading His Word and worship, keeps Jesus at the centre of everything else I do. But it takes practice and discipline.

As you grow and develop in the things of God, you come to an understanding that even if you miss your planned time for whatever reason, you can converse with Him throughout the day. The Father doesn't condemn us. God is a good, good Father. He graciously welcomes us to enjoy the time spent with Him in fellowship and communion.

We should not allow the colour of our skin or the standards set by others to define who we are. The way we see ourselves can be influenced by our early experiences in life, whether it's been a good start or not. When we're born again, our true identity is in Christ alone. God sees us as His masterpiece. The dictionary defines a 'masterpiece' as a work of outstanding artistry, skill, or workmanship. The Bible says, *"For we are His workmanship [His own master work, a work of art], created in Christ Jesus [reborn from above—spiritually transformed, renewed, ready to be used] for good works, which God prepared [for us] beforehand [taking paths which He set]"* (Ephesians 2:10).

It's taken a while for me to see myself the way God sees me in Christ: He sees me as a new creation. In Christ I am in right standing with God. I am loved unconditionally by God, and His love helps me to love others unconditionally. My new recreated spirit is the real me. *"Therefore, if anyone is in Christ, he is a new creation; old things have passed away; behold, all things have become new"* (2 Corinthians 5:17 NKJV).

The Bible teaches we were created by the Almighty God with three distinct but not separate parts. We are a spirit (the REAL YOU), with a mind (a free will and emotions), and we live in a temporal or physical body. Our spirit man possesses a body and mind that are linked to the earthly and supernatural realms.

When we know who we are in Christ, we will discover the importance of truly resting in Him. We rest in His promises by faith, knowing He has good plans for our lives. When we strive to achieve or earn His love, we put pressure on ourselves. Our bodies are of great significance to the Father. *"Do you not know that your body is a temple of the Holy Spirit who is within you, whom you have [received as a gift] from God, and that you* are not your own [property]? *[20] You were bought with a price, honor and glorify God with your body"* (1 Corinthians 6:19-20).

We are owners and stewards of our bodies, and this makes us personally responsible for doing our part. The body has the capacity to heal itself when our immune system is functioning correctly.

There are two important points to consider:

1. Disease can be in our bodies for many years without us knowing
2. Whenever the Holy Spirit prompts us, He is trying to alert us to take some action

### *What is stress?*

Research tells us that 95% of our visits to the doctor are for causes of stress related illnesses. Many Christians experience burn out because of overload. Positive stress is called eustress, and negative stress is actually distress. Positive stress is things we believe we can cope with while negative stress is those things we perceive are out of our control. According to an article, I read:

> *A stressor is anything that causes the release of stress hormones. There are two broad categories of stressors—physical stressors and psychological stressors. Major life changes can affect us adversely and is an example of negative stress. When we are anxious or fearful, the brain secretes the wrong kind of chemicals that can harm our bodies and affect our mental health and emotions in a negative way.* (BBC.co.uk Science 2013).

Stress is also emotional. It can manifest itself in the loss of a loved one or a significant experience, anxiety, anger or depression.

## Useful tips

- Too much stress can have a detrimental effect spiritually, emotionally, psychologically and physically

- Keeping a good balance of the good stress hormones is important
- Don't ignore signs and symptoms in your body
- Never underestimate gut feelings or intuition

## Exercises

Stress is a huge complex subject. To help you identify some of the stressors, you may have, please answer the following questions.

### Identify things that cause you stress:

_____

_____

_____

_____

_____

_____

_____

_____

_____

_____

_____

_____

_____

_____

_____

_____

_____

_____

_____

_____

_____

_____

_____

_____

_____

How can you manage stress better? (It might be a case of just saying 'no' to a request that is not urgent or important)

_____
_____
_____
_____
_____
_____
_____
_____
_____
_____

What support do you need to help you achieve this goal? (It could be getting support from someone)

_____
_____
_____
_____
_____
_____
_____
_____

How do I know I have arrived at my goal? (Give a date of when you want to complete your task, for example within a week or a month. Remember to be realistic)

_____
_____
_____
_____
_____
_____
_____

**Action—what are the next steps for you?**

_____
_____
_____
_____
_____
_____
_____
_____
_____
_____

## *My Next Steps*

In a sentence or two, write down a personal goal. Example:

My goal is: To prioritise and use my time effectively on a daily basis

_____
_____
_____
_____
_____
_____
_____
_____
_____

Think about how you can prioritise your time. What tasks fall into the following categories:

1. 'Important and urgent'
2. 'Non-important and non-urgent.'

## Important and urgent

_____
_____
_____
_____
_____
_____
_____
_____
_____

## Non-important and non-urgent

_____
_____
_____
_____
_____
_____
_____
_____

# STEP 2—MANAGE THE TRANSITION

## Motherhood

A mother means more than giving birth to children. A mother demonstrates commitment, love and care, comes what may. It's being woken up in the middle of the night because your child had a nightmare. It's being inconvenienced, and knowing when to put their needs before yours and, actually, it's learning to enjoy them. It's being there when they fall down and need a bandage after grazing a knee, even if it's not needed, and saying "there, there, never mind." It's coming alongside and affirming them, and being their greatest cheerleader, ally and the list goes on.

I get defensive when we are classed as 'adoptive mothers.' For goodness sakes, a mum is a mum irrespective of how they came to have children. In fact, my children disliked being called adopted. They told me it made them feel 'different'. I reminded them they are not 'a special case' but chosen and handpicked from others. In the same way, when we come to faith, our adoption in Christ means that we are part of Him. The Sovereign God is Abba or Daddy Father. This means He truly loves us. Through Jesus' suffering, death and resurrection, we have true Sonship.

> The Sovereign God is Abba or Daddy Father.
> This means He truly loves us.

I had always wanted to be a mother. Growing up in a large family, as one of the older children, was my preparation for motherhood. Very early on in my childhood, I enjoyed playing 'dolls houses', which I made out of different types of materials. I also enjoyed playing with my favourite doll's tea set. It looked like real china, a present from my great Aunt Mary, with whom I often spent the holidays.

There was a large cupboard at the top of our stairs, along the landing. It was painted black, and naturally, we referred to it as the 'black place'. Essentially, it was my hideaway, although I was too big to fit into it. I'm not sure who nominated me to be in charge of this play area. My siblings had to ask my permission to join in. Most of the toys were kept in there.

I spent many hours in my imaginary world and copied what I saw happening around me. I had big dreams and imagined myself married with seven sons. As one of four girls, I found it easier to get along with boys, probably because I didn't have to compete with them.

Eil and I helped Mum look after our younger siblings. We observed all that Mum did. She taught us how to hold newborn babies. Those were the days when they wrapped new born babies in layers of sheets and blankets to keep them warm. We learnt to change nappies, wash and dress our siblings, and made up bottles of SMA baby milk. I remember quite vividly the small stool our mother had bought specially for us to use. We were still young, and she kept a watchful eye on us. I recall the numerous times Mum would shout out, "Who wants to feed the baby?" By that time they had reached the stage to have solid food.

Eagerly, I would run ahead of Eil and promptly sat down on the stool before she could. "Have you washed your hands?" Mum would ask. I replied, 'Yes' but it wasn't always the case. I didn't particularly like the taste of mashed potatoes and vegetables that she prepared. I was more interested in the puddings. My favourite was Farley Rusks made with hot milk or the apple puree she used from the jar. Needless to say, I ate most of the food, and the poor babies ended up screaming because they were still hungry. Mum didn't say much but looked at me with a wide grin because she knew what was happening.

I suspect getting married at the age of 26 was old in the 1980s, but I certainly didn't relish the idea of getting pregnant straight away. There was more than enough to occupy my time.

By the time we were in our late twenties, we were ready to have children of our own, but there were complications. Tests and procedures were carried out but there were no medical reasons for infertility. My gynaecologist, a stern looking consultant from the 'old school,' told me removing fibroids would give a better chance of getting pregnant. I agreed to it and she carried out a myomectomy to remove the small fibroids but it didn't improve our chances. My biological clock was ticking loudly and my maternal instincts were increasing. My hopes were dashed each time I received the negative results at the end of monthly cycles.

Often, when Tony and I had days out or wherever we saw families with children, I would observe the interaction between them. On the surface it looked as if everything was perfect. Even though I knew this wasn't a reality I still imagined myself with children. Everywhere we went we were surrounded by children. We have many godchildren and we still get asked to be godparents, a responsibility we don't take lightly. We have lots of nieces and nephews who have had their own children, and the family is still growing.

Years ago, a mother asked us to have her young daughter for the week-end. Apparently, her daughter was obsessed with me. It wasn't a case that I saw her daughter regularly but every day she spoke to her mum about me. In an effort to get rid of her obsession, we made the arrangements, and she spent the week-end. It turns out it didn't cure her at all. I imagine that she grew out of it after a while.

We didn't know many childless couples in our circle of friends. Obviously, there were those who didn't want children of their own and others who simply couldn't have them. There were times I felt isolated and envied women I saw that were pregnant. I actually related to women in the Bible who were married and childless. In Bible days, childlessness was seen as a public disgrace. Women were made to feel like outcasts. They were taunted and oppressed by other women as though God had somehow punished them.

The Bible takes us into the private moments of women such as Sara, Abraham's wife, and Anna who became Samuel, the prophet's mother. These women prayed for children, and after many years of waiting, children were born in their advanced years. I saw these women as resilient because they didn't give up hope in a faithful God.

It's easier to criticise others when we don't understand. We become judge and jury when we don't know the facts and make assumptions. Childless couples are seen as if it isn't God's will for them to have children but there are many reasons for infertility.

Our spoken words and belief system can bring either life or death. For a long time, I had said "There's no way I'm going through that painful labour stuff. I would prefer to have my children given to me." I had built up an image in me that childbirth could be long and painful and I didn't want to have that experience, although I knew women whose experience of childbirth was pain free and easy. Having a 'perfect' baby at the end is priceless. I know that life is precious, and that children are gifts from God.

It's a natural process for children to play 'mummies and daddies' and we weren't any different. Growing up my sisters and I put cushions under our clothes and pretended to be pregnant. But for some reason, I just couldn't see myself pregnant. I visualized my children were given to me. I even dreamt that I had twins, a boy, and girl and named them Jason and Jenny.

There is a saying there is no gain without pain. There is always some kind of price to be paid. Whether the price is walking through a process or preparing to achieve a personal or spiritual goal, there is a cost, but the prize is well worth it.

The time came when we wanted children, but it wasn't happening. Father God gave me a precise Word: "He makes the barren woman to be a homemaker and a joyful mother of (*spiritual*) children." Praise the Lord! (Psalms 113:9). I held onto this promise for 21 years.

## Navigating the challenges of a new family

### *Preparing for adoption*

Under normal circumstances, we don't choose our families. However, in this technological age, scientists have found ways to modify man's genetic makeup to suit people's preferences. Parents can choose the sex of their children and the colour of their eyes. One can argue, whether it is right or wrong to tamper with God's creation. We are told in scripture that God instructed the human race to replenish, have dominion over the earth and over all living things. However, His perfect will is for children to be raised in a marriage union of a man and woman. Children need Godly and loving homes, with good role models.

We made enquiries about adoption through one of our friends. She was an experienced social worker who worked for the City

Council. She advised us to use a private adoption agency, as in her view it was less complicated and would achieve the same outcomes.

We began our journey to find the right children by thinking ahead. We knew that children who came from the care system would need our full attention. I made plans to relinquish my role as director and chair of the charity organization we had started. At the time the project attracted major funding to renovate the church annex, and eventually, the centre moved to its own premises.

Flicking through the TV channels one day, I came across a Christian adoption agency and made enquiries. Tony and I had previously discussed our next steps. Pretty soon we were on our way to becoming parents. Instantly, we clicked with our social worker. She had a very bubbly personality and had, herself, been a pastor's wife. She understood the pressures of ministry and was able to relate to our situation. We became good friends.

The adoption process was stressful due to the amount of work involved, and the fact that we were still busy working in full time jobs. We attended training sessions with other potential adopters. The meetings with our social worker were kept in our home. Each week she would review the tasks she had set for us to do. By Christmas of that year, we were 'approved adopters.' Our social worker relocated, and her replacement worked with us for a number of years, until the agency was no longer involved. Although an experienced worker, she was a little out of touch with reality.

## Matching process

The next stage was to match us with children. We wanted two, a boy and girl, who were siblings: from birth up to 5 years old. We relished the idea of adopting babies because we thought it might be easier for them to adapt to a new way of life.

Hours were spent viewing photographs and profiles of children, as soon as the courts approved them for adoption. We knew that God would lead us to the right children, but at that time, it just wasn't happening soon enough for us.

Working hard and still busy taking on other projects, we reached the point where Tony felt we should abandon the idea and get on with our own lives. The social worker was losing patience and became quite stern towards us. She asked if we still intended to adopt but I couldn't see life without children.

Tony agreed to continue our search but, intuitively, I knew he wasn't fully persuaded. However, he supported my desire to become a mum.

The social worker continued to send photographs of children and their family history. The children, we found, were much older than what we wanted. She was annoyed when we discounted the children she felt would be a good match for us. In her estimation time was of the essence: it was coming up to almost a year since we were approved adopters. The process became mechanical and insensitive.

Then it all happened in a flash. The photograph from the adoption magazine was sent for us to consider. There were two children, a boy and a girl, very similar to my dream. Jenny and her brother were older than our ideal, but their faces told a story. They were indeed 'perfect' for us.

From the sketchy information, we weren't made fully aware of the impact of the children's difficulties and the struggles we might face later.

There were gaps in the children's history, but somehow, we weren't given the opportunity to thoroughly explore those gaps before adoption. After all, we were dealing with real people and not statistics.

A panel meeting was held with professionals from both local authorities. Due to the children's Mixed Race identity, it was felt that, ideally, they would be best placed with White or Mixed Race parents. Our social worker didn't consider there was ever an issue with the fact that we were Black. The panel members came to a swift decision that it was a 'perfect' match and they agreed that we progress to the final stage.

## Children's background

The children were in care because of neglect, one of the four categories of abuse. But neglect is grossly underestimated. It is a major area of concern because it affects all aspects of emotional, physical, sexual and psychological abuse.

The children lived with their extended family and were well known to Social Care.

The children's foster carer had concerns about some of the behaviours Jason was exhibiting. Jason was sent for an assessment by a psychologist. In his report, the psychologist described the family as 'living on the margins of society and having a dysfunctional and chaotic lifestyle. Children living in the household were in and out of care.'

At that time the psychologist's report had not been shared with the foster carer, and she was unaware it even existed. She was surprised that, given the background of Jenny and Jason, they were the only children who came to her without therapy; and she had fostered many children over the years, including children of Mixed Race, Black, and White.

Jason recalled the story and told me: "The police didn't dare to venture down our street." They were used to seeing police vans and fire brigades. The law became something that they disliked, vehemently. They considered the law more of an enemy than for their protection. Jason remembers, on one occasion when he was staying with his aunt, there was a knock on the door. A social worker had come to take him away. As he screamed, his aunt promised to get him back.

The real issue for us was the likelihood of how the children's traumatic past would affect them in time to come, but no one discussed it with us. It was as though a magic wand would be waved and everything would simply fall into place.

Once the children settled, we saw changes in their behaviours that no doubt had been suppressed for some time. Tony ended up making further explorations. He found out how the children had fended for themselves by stealing to survive. From a very early age Jason had become a carer for his sister.

The children's anxieties were often acted out in their behaviours. Research shows that children with traumatic experiences, in their early years, are more prone to have higher levels of anxiety and stress more than other children. Our concerns led us to take Jason to see the community paediatrician for an assessment, due to the trauma he had experienced. He was diagnosed with Post-Traumatic Stress Disorder and Attention Deficit Hyperactivity Disorder (ADHD).

Up until this point, Jenny was overlooked completely. It was obvious to us that since both children had lived under the same conditions, Jenny would have similar needs. Many years passed before Jenny was diagnosed and therapy came far too late for both of them.

Jason remembers when they were taken away by the police who arrived at the home wearing riot uniforms. They were frightened and were carried away kicking and screaming. Jason recalls in detail the last time he saw his family. Jenny's memories are sparse, but Jason remembers more.

They were separated when they were put into care. Jenny was unable to cope without her brother, and would constantly cry for him. They were eventually placed together with the same carer.

Tony and I tried to speak positively about their birth mum and the challenges she faced in her life. At the same time, we wanted the children to know that their early years' experiences had an impact on their behaviours. Jenny showed no interest in hearing about her birth mum, but Jason was more protective of her and wanted to know why she gave them up. Sadly, their birth mum passed away, so Jason would never hear the explanation from her lips.

## Introduction meetings

When we arrived on our first visit to see the children, they hid behind the settees at their foster home and wanted us to find them. Jenny could be easily seen, while Jason was a little more creative. Their foster mum was very supportive and gave us the tips she had used with them. She described Jason as extremely boisterous and even though he would hit his little sister, he loved and cared for her. Jenny was very girly: one of her favourite colours was pink. Jason was crazy about cars; something he had in common with his new Dad.

As part of the introductions, we had to drive up the motorway to spend time with the children. We stayed at a nearby hotel so that we could see our children each day. We took them to school and back and enjoyed a family trip to the zoo. We had a great time getting to know each other. We prepared our children for bedtime and read their favourite stories. Their foster mum had taken them to church regularly, so they were used to saying prayers at bed time. We were pleasantly surprised how they took it all in their stride, and how much they were at ease with us.

Tony and I had talked about what they would call us. He suggested we take it a step at a time and sure enough they called us 'Mummy and Daddy.' It was beautiful to my ears. Father God had gone before us and prepared their hearts, I imagine, with a little help from their foster mum.

At their old school, Jason was in the infants and Jenny in the nursery. Jason proudly introduced his new Daddy to his friends. Jenny clung tightly to her foster mum pretending to ignore me, but she was only weighing me up. Her little grin would then appear as she emerged from behind her foster mum.

They were popular with teachers and children alike, and on the last day they were given gifts. It was a tearful parting for them, especially Jason. The school did not have any problems with the children. We witnessed how genuinely the children were loved by the teachers and children alike. There were good reports all around. Jason was very popular and Jenny a shy, quiet and reserved little girl. It was eye opening to see how well the school they left behind supported them. I couldn't understand why there was such a contrast to the new school they would soon attend near home.

Jenny had beautiful golden brown hair and Jason's was brown and tightly curled. He had a mischievous grin on his face, and Jenny's smile lit up her face with her hazel brown eyes that glowed in the sun. She was, and she is still beautiful. They both are beautiful looking children. Almost immediately Jason asked if we would be changing their first names, but we had no plans to do so.

We put an album together for the children to introduce them to their new home and extended families. It helped to familiarise the children with their new environment before they arrived. The social workers were impressed with the way things were going and were keen to move things on. They arranged for the children, accompanied by their foster mum, to visit their new home.

Over that week, things went relatively well much to the surprise of the social workers. Tony dealt with an incident where Jason was reluctant to do something. He kept a firm boundary and Jason eventually gave in. It was at that point that I knew we were in for an interesting journey.

It was at that point that I knew we were in for an interesting journey.

## A new beginning

The children said goodbye to their neighbours and school friends. It was a difficult transition for them. Jason bravely said goodbye to his friends but cried about leaving his best friend behind.

In May 2003, we brought our children home. Jenny cried for her foster mum all the way down the motorway. There was nothing we could do to console her but, interestingly, the moment Jason told her she was giving everyone a headache, she stopped crying. Here we were with our 'twins' just like the dream I had many years ago. I was so elated to be a mother at last.

The children's social worker gave us their life story books but left us with the impression they should be put out of sight. Each album had photographs of them when they were babies and family members they had left behind. The social worker used simple terms to describe the reasons why the children had come into care and adoption. However, when our adoption agency was ready to do life story work, they were unhappy with the way the books were presented. In their view, they were merely picture albums and there were some inaccuracies.

Local authorities have a statutory duty to create life story books for all adopted children but the ways in which these are compiled can differ enormously. Life story books are used to help children understand and come to terms with their past. They should contain detailed information on what is known about the children's history and background.

Research suggests that involving adoptive parents is crucial to the creation of children's life story work, as it involves the past and current experiences of the child.

Jason was the first to have his life story work with our adoption worker. We were unaware of how important it was for one of us to be present. Reading between the lines we felt uninvited by the social worker and left our son in her care.

Our son left our home with the social worker as a happy, contented child. He returned home a highly traumatised child. The social worker explained how certain things had upset Jason. She didn't appear to be aware of the impact the session had on him. It had brought back painful memories of his past and triggered other memories that he had blocked out but were still deeply entrenched within him. He described to me the gory details of the violence he had witnessed as a small child. At this time Jason was about 8 years old. It had been the first time he had opened up to me in this way. What he told me was not recorded anywhere in the documents. I held him tightly in my arms as he sat on my lap. His tears came from deep within his heart. From that moment on, we decided that we would use everything in our power to avoid a similar experience for Jenny when she was ready for her life story work to be done. We kept this promise. Fortunately, Jason didn't have any further contact with the same social worker.

There were many precious moments in our first few weeks that turned into the months and years. Our social worker visited us regularly for a while, and this continued sporadically until the children were in their early teens.

The children settled fairly well, but things weren't as they appeared on the surface. Jenny started at the local nursery school and Jason at the infants. Both schools were within walking distance, but I drove the children to school and back.

Evidently, one of us was needed at home for the sake of the children. We agreed that I would take a year out from my job, even though I couldn't get paid maternity leave: at that time there was no provision for adoptive mothers to be paid. I felt this was a discrimination against 'adoptive' mothers. After researching the policies of other public sector providers, I found that there were some anomalies in my organization. I made a case to the Human Resources department, challenging the policy and as a consequence, my employers agreed there should be the same entitlement of paid leave for 'adoptive' mothers. Even though I wouldn't benefit from the changes made, because the agreement came after my leave had started, at least I knew others would benefit. Our income had reduced from two full time salaries to one part time salary. By then my husband, Tony had been made redundant from his job and was working for an agency on a temporary contract. Even though we learnt to manage on what we had, Father God provided in ways we didn't imagine.

There were hiccups at school for Jason. From the behaviour he was exhibiting, we knew he was missing his best friend. When we contacted the boy's family at first they seemed eager for them to meet up. Sadly for Jason, after a while, the family no longer responded to our invitations. I believe Jason's best friend had moved on with his life.

One of my fondest memories was the time when Jason asked: "Am I from your tummy?" His little face stared up at me, anxiously waiting for my response. It took me by surprise, but I knew Jason needed reassuring. Stooping down to his level I told him, "You know that you didn't come from my tummy, Jason. But you come from my heart!" His little face lit up as if to say, 'well that's settled now.' and off he went to play. I meant every word I said.

Jason got into trouble almost every day. From then on Jenny had a worried expression on her face. I got into the routine of picking up Jenny first, which gave just enough time to collect Jason. On our way there, Jenny would regularly ask, "I wonder what sort of day Jason has had today, Mummy?' I would reply, "Let's hope he's had a good day." We wanted to 'nip his behaviour in the bud,' so I enlisted the support of our social worker. She accompanied me to see the head teacher one day after school. In our meeting, Jenny sat on my lap as we talked. The social worker gave the headmaster a lesson on empathy about children like Jason. From then on he seemed more accepting and made allowances for Jason.

At first, the social worker complimented our parenting skills. There was nothing she wouldn't do to support us. But as more problems emerged, there was a decline in her efforts to help. We noticed an undertone of disapproval in her expression. She had high expectations that the coping strategies she had given us would work, but those strategies were only a case of 'trial and error'. Later on we were blamed for the children's behaviours, and we noticed how conveniently the children's history was pushed to one side.

Everyone knew how bright Jason really was, but when he had finished his work in class, because he had time on his hands, he would become disruptive. We saw how he flourished in his reading and writing. Parents were encouraged to read regularly with their child before school started. Instead of using phonics to help with reading, Tony taught Jason a different method which he found more beneficial. The change in Jason's reading was dramatic. Soon he was an avid reader and enjoyed reading on his own.

We joined book clubs and were regular visitors to the local library. Jenny took longer with her reading and writing. They both had private tuition in Maths and English, and I supported the children at home. Jenny's dainty writing style spoke volumes to me. Her writing and drawing were so small it was as though she was afraid to use up the whole sheet of paper. I implemented methods that helped them to learn in a fun-loving way.

Jason progressed to junior school. From then onwards, he was put on what they called 'regular reports.' He was labelled as a problem child by children and teachers alike. Jason was blamed for anything and everything that went wrong in school, even when he wasn't there! He spent most of his time in either detention or exclusions.

When Jenny finished the infant school, we moved her with her brother to a new junior school. We were doing it for the right reasons. Somehow it seemed to be the worse decision we ever made, or so we thought. Jenny was looking forward to moving to junior school with her friends and, naturally, she was upset by the prospect of not seeing them again. We made sure she kept in regular contact. It wasn't easy for her to keep the friends she had made. The result would be that she would have to make new friends all over again, and we didn't know the impact it would have on her. A new start was what we intended for the children, but from that moment on Jenny lived in her brother's shadow.

Jason spent most of his time in the head teacher's office. He displayed some of the characteristics of ADHD as he found it difficult to sit still, especially in assemblies. By that time we were already attending many school meetings arranged by the head teacher, because of Jason's behaviour. He got into fights and showed inappropriate behaviour towards others. I recall the time she phoned and said, 'Do you know how much of my time your son takes up?" I'm not sure what she expected us to do, but we were put under great duress for Jason's behaviour to change. On reflection I can now see that the teachers were naive: I came to the conclusion that they just didn't understand.

One day Jason came into my room. As he sat down, he covered his head with the hood from the jumper he was wearing. He looked forlorn and ashamed. He asked, "Mummy, why am I like this?" I reassured him that it wasn't his fault; he wasn't to blame himself for what had happened to him in his early life.

Jason's behaviour became more extreme as he got older. Our son's behavioural difficulties manifested themselves in low-level behaviour from name calling to hitting other children. In contrast, as he behaved impeccably at home and responded to the firm boundaries we had in place, we couldn't understand some of what we were told by the teachers.

The trouble at school continued, and we were at our wit's end. We resorted to smacking Jason. The next day in school assembly his head teacher threatened to report him to us again. Jason innocently replied that he would get a smack from his Dad if he got into trouble. The head teacher contacted us to let us know she had reported the incident to Social Care. Soon we received a call and were visited by them.

A Child Protection enquiry was made, and the next thing we knew we were being asked to take the children to the children's hospital. Examination and interviews were conducted with the children and the social worker visited us afterwards. Even though we were put under pressure by the school, we accepted it wasn't something we would resort to do again, and the case was closed. It was a distressing experience for all of us, especially for Jenny. We contacted our adoption social worker. By this time, we had a new social worker. She was supportive and understood the enormous pressure that was put on us by the school. We later found out that although the social worker had closed the case, she had arranged for Tony to speak with the Child Protection police officer.

While no action was taken, it left us with a very unpleasant taste. Our social worker sent a letter of complaint to her manager but there was no response.

Looking back, we had looked forward to a fresh start at this new school. It was out in the country and the journey there was pleasant. Once again, however, the new move came with new challenges. As the challenges continued, we looked for more solutions. The older the children became, the more acute their needs were.

We were one of only three Black families. Many of the parents were professional people, who complained about minor things Jason did. We involved an educational psychologist who arranged an assessment in school. In the report, the assessor wrote, 'Jason looked out of place.' I wasn't at all impressed and asked what was meant by this. I don't recall how they responded, but from then on, they found out we were assertive parents and would challenge them if we felt there had been any discrimination against Jason.

Even though Jason received mentorship support in school, there were still exclusions, which became longer. This had a snowball effect, and our son was faced with a permanent exclusion. I had a few days to write a report in his defence.

Eil signposted me to the Parenting Partnership. Their help was invaluable. We didn't manage to change the head teacher's mind, but a compromise was reached. Moving Jason to alternative education provision, where he received one-to-one tuition wasn't ideal, but we agreed it was better than being permanently excluded.

Everywhere Jason went teachers and pupils commented on his academic abilities. He was a gifted child, and very likeable but this was overshadowed by his behaviour.

As Jason got older, his risk-taking behaviours increased. He started staying out, without our knowledge, and returning home in the early hours of the morning. It was as though it was an addiction to him. He was looking for his identity and was probably grieving his loss from the past he remembered. Jenny silently observed him, and there were times she told him off over the things he was doing. We sought for ways to help him.

Eil had her own practice, and was running parenting courses; one of which was called Triple P, which stands for Positive Parenting Programme. It was eye opening. I went home from one of the sessions and implemented some of the strategies straightway. Examples of the strategies I used are given in the addendum in Appendix 2.

Tony and I went on training courses to help us understand the reasons the children behaved in the way they did. One of the courses, which left a lasting impression on us, was "I Can't Dance. Don't Ask Me." It was like the psychologist leading the training was reading our minds. A large group of parents and teachers attended, and one of Jason's school teachers accompanied us.

The quality of the course was good and it answered a lot of our questions. We learnt so much. Enthusiastically, we all nodded our heads to what was being said. We all found ourselves saying, "My child does that" and "Okay—that's the reason they behave like that." We left deeply motivated to try out more of the strategies that were recommended. There was a sigh of relief when we learnt we weren't the only ones going through this ordeal.

We attended more training events for adoptive families, which were facilitated by the Support after Adoption Team, but this didn't go down well with the children. They felt it was for abnormal people, and didn't like going. We had to do a lot of persuading before they reluctantly, went with us and joined in with the children's activities.

The parents' sessions gave us opportunity to network with other adopters. There were further revelations of families from other parts of the country who were given therapeutic support for the whole family. All sorts of services were available that we weren't getting from our local council. We had been short changed: it felt so unfair and disproportionate.

Over many years, we sought funding to support our children's therapeutic needs, through writing letters to senior managers of Social Care. We also gained the support of our local MP. When we asked Social Care for help, they told us nothing could be done unless the children were in their care. We couldn't believe what we were hearing.

At last, we were able to find the right therapist who was recommended by Eil. We were tired of waiting and paid privately for our son to be seen. He got on well with the psychotherapist, who was extremely knowledgeable and thorough. He took the time to get to know our family and spoke frankly and honestly with us. He was the only professional that made any sense to us. There was one thing we had in common—our experiences of discrimination. He had been a social worker and understood the pressure of working in a care system that was under-resourced.

To experience a change of scenery, we would go away for most of the school holidays. We had days out and travelled to different parts of the country and abroad. We noticed the positive impact it had on the children. They enjoyed family holidays away and always thanked us for taking them. We noticed a sense of value and appreciation blossoming in them.

In our second year with the children, we took them to Disney World in America. This was our first family trip abroad. The children were buzzing with excitement. It was the first time they had been on an aeroplane. It was a joy to see how happy they were. We stayed at one of Disney's hotels. Even there things didn't go to plan. Somehow Jason managed, without us knowing, to fill his pockets with items that weren't paid for. He really believed they belonged to him! We marched him back to the store to return the items. That episode didn't dampen their spirits, though. The children were in their element, and we enjoyed our fortnight together in the sunshine: the beach, the scenery and the different rides. It was a great adventure for them.

I recall another incident when Jason and Jenny persuaded children they'd just met to take money that didn't belong to them. They'd made up all kinds of stories, but the truth eventually came out. They returned it, but Tony reported the incident to a policeman with a view they would learn from the experience and not repeat the behaviour. The policeman gave them a good lecturing about what the consequences of breaking the law could mean. They showed great remorse over the incident.

There were also some touching moments. I recall a time when Tony had taken the children to the DIY store. It was good breathing space for me to put my feet up with a cup of coffee. They were all in the store together when shortly afterwards Tony moved to another aisle. He was unaware the children were not with him. Moments after, the children found him. They were distressed and in tears, believing he had left them in the store. It frightened them. Tony reassured the children that this wasn't the case. He had inadvertently moved to the aisle thinking they were with him. He promised he would never leave them.

> He promised he would never leave them.

When they got to secondary school, the children's behaviours became more challenging but this was outside of the home. Gradually, the behaviours impacted on our home and social lives. They were more drawn to people with backgrounds that were akin to the experiences of their formative years.

Over the ensuing years, our daughter silently observed her brother's behaviours. She kept her own emotional difficulties to herself until in her early teens. When it did come out it was like an erupting volcano. Jenny went from being a quiet and shy child to a completely different person. She was now staying out until the early hours of the morning.

As responsible parents, we did what we believed was right and reported the children to the police, whenever they went missing. We felt it was for their protection. The police would come round, and sometimes our home was searched for the children. Having the presence of the police in our home was traumatic. It increased our stress levels, but the children seemed oblivious to the impact it was having on us. It was the 'norm' that they remembered. It seemed that this was the way they were wired, and it would be impossible to change them. It was only by the mercies of God that they were not abducted or harmed.

Whenever he was excluded from school, Jason spent much of his time at home or in my office at work. He absolutely loved spending time with me and seeing my staff, who spoilt him with sweets and gifts.

When he was in alternative education, Jason passed his Standard Attainment Test with flying colours. Outside of school, Jenny achieved top awards in ballet, tap and drama. She performed at the Arts Theatre in front of large audiences. The ballet company she performed with was featured on the front page of the local press. Both children enjoyed swimming, basketball, football, the brownies, and cadets. It helped develop their social skills, but there were also times when they found it difficult to interact with other children and Jason, in particular, would get into trouble.

The children found mainstream schools a challenge even though they got into the best church schools we could find. They continued education in alternative settings, where class sizes were smaller. Jenny achieved good results and went on to college for a while, as did Jason. They gained reasonable qualifications. The journey continues as Jenny and Jason begin their own journeys towards finding their divine purpose and destiny.

# STEP 3—SEE FROM DIFFERENT PERSPECTIVES

## What angle are you seeing from?

Johari Windows is a theory to help us find out how we perceive ourselves and the way we are perceived by others. It's a diagnostic tool to develop self-awareness, help with personal development and improve communications and interpersonal relationships. These areas are built on trust.

Children with early years' trauma have tremendous trust and attachment issues. Attachment is how we build relationships. Those attachments can be healthy or unhealthy. My children didn't have the emotional ability to differentiate between healthy and unhealthy attachments. This created vulnerabilities, which sometimes resulted in them getting into difficulties. A good example of this is that they find it hard to keep promises, yet they are devastated when promises are broken by others.

Trust is built when we disclose information about ourselves to others, and they in turn disclose about themselves.

| 1 open/free area | 2 blind area |
|---|---|
| 3 hidden area | 4 unknown area |

The four areas to the Johari Window are given in the above diagram. The first is an open and free area. It looks at what we want to share in the public arena, such as feelings, behaviour, attitude, and views known by ourselves and others (Luff 2017).

In the next area, we identify our *blind spots* by looking at what is known by others in the group but unknown by ourselves. The third is our *hidden area*. We sometimes wear façades to protect ourselves and keep things hidden from others to disguise our feelings. Finally, the *unknown area* gives us the opportunity to discover ourselves and others.

From a young age, my children were very skilled at keeping things hidden. Either it was hoarding food or not telling the truth. It seemed to be woven into their makeup. They fabricated stories to cover up their tracks. Sometimes their stories just didn't add up, but they persisted with them, nonetheless. These stories could be so convincing that there were times when even I doubted myself, about what I knew. I was so amazed at how quickly the words came out of their mouths, without them even batting an eyelid. It was their survival instinct and defence mechanism kicking in.

We would try different strategies to get to the truth. Years ago, when Jason was less economical with the truth, I told him, "Adults can see when children aren't speaking the truth." He asked me: "How? "It's written all over their faces," I replied. Jason quickly ran to look at himself in the mirror, "I don't see anything" he said. "Only adults can see it," I replied. He looked perplexed. I added, "By your expressions." I think it left him with something to think about.

Have you ever felt you have been listened to? How does it make you feel? Often, we focus on what we want to say, and ignore this important part of communication. Listening is a skill. The skill is to listen, at a deeper level, to someone without thinking of how you will respond. It is a skill that develops with practice over time.

From very early on, Jenny and Jason learnt to trust in different ways and at different times. Whenever they felt secure, they opened up. Whenever I promised I wouldn't get cross, even if I didn't agree with their actions, they found it easier to tell me things. I repeatedly reassured them they were loved and demonstrated it. I would open my arms towards them, and in turn they would run into my arms. There were times when I showed my own vulnerability. I remember an occasion when I told them about my own imperfections and some of the things I did when I was their age. Jason replied 'You're very clever Mummy. You know just how to get to the truth, don't you?'

As young adults, depending on which one I'm talking to, they will say, "I'll tell you, if you promise not to tell Jason or Jenny that I've told you, Mum." I smile because I know they will eventually open up to each other.

Children need to know we all make bad choices at some point in our lives. Change happens when we are willing to make adjustments. Learning from our mistakes has the potential to make a better future, but we have to take the steps to grow. Otherwise, the same behaviour is repeated, and we end up saying, "If only I had listened", or words to that effect.

In the next section, I have shared the children's feelings and views about care and adoption. At the time of writing, Jason was going through long periods in residential care and youth detentions. Jenny had experienced intermittent periods with the care system. By God's grace, we had managed the stormy and choppy waters even though we were separated from each other. In His timing, Father God brought us back together.

## Jason's perspective

In 2003, my whole life changed forever. I was taken from the custody of my birth mum and put into Social Care. At the time I didn't understand, but I remember it as if it happened yesterday. On the day, I was spending some time with my Aunty Dawn and we had just come back from McDonalds. I was playing with my Lego in the front room of her flat, when there was a knock at the door. When aunty opened it, there was a woman standing there with some police officers. The woman introduced herself as a social worker and told my aunty that she was there to take me. Aunty tried to fight for me, but due to the police presence, there was nothing she could do. I recall her repeatedly saying to me, "Don't worry. It'll be okay. I'll see you soon." Little did I know that this would be the last time I saw her and I would never ever see my birth mum again.

To be completely honest, the foster placement I got put in was not bad at all. At first, it was just the carer, her son and me. A day or two later, my younger sister came to live there as well. Our lives were 100% different from what we were previously used to. We had someone who was actually looking after us; food in our stomachs; clothes on our back and a safe, stable environment to live in. I had joined a school and my sister a nursery. We had also started going to church and Sunday School because our carer was a strong Christian. We also went on regular trips with the agency she worked for. For once in our lives, things were normal.

We had been under Social Care for about two years before we were introduced to Mum and Dad. I can't remember the very first time meeting them, but after a while, we used to go out with them often and visited their home a number of times. At one stage, leading up to the adoption, we used to see them near enough every day.

May 12th, 2003 was the date we left foster care and moved in with our parents (Tony and Hyacinth). I was almost 6, and my sister was 4, it was her birthday. All the neighbours came out to say goodbye and wish us the best. It took ages for us to calm down and get in the car. I calmed down after a while; my sister cried all the way down the motorway and for the majority of the journey.

I would say we settled into life with our new family fairly quickly. We met the rest of the family and everyone was nice to us. We'd both started new schools, and I got on well there and made some friends as well. Everything at home was good, and there were no major problems. It was as if we'd been in the family from day one. The only thing was my behaviour at school, apart from that there was nothing else. It was when I got older and started to learn things about my birth family that the real problems started.

2012 was when things at home really started to go downhill for me. I was in constant trouble with the law, and this attracted the attention of Social Care. I was on multiple Youth Offending Team Orders but they made no difference to me, and I continued to get into trouble until I got dumped in a residential school. It was basically a boarding school/children's home/secure unit. I absolutely hated it there and absconded, every opportunity I got. After a while, they got fed up with me and refused to accept me back, so it was care home to care home from there, until I got sent to a youth institution.

I was there for just under two years before I went to live back with my parents. I had changed a lot over my years away from home, and so had my parents. They had become more relaxed and treated me more as an adult. When I came back home, it was like clockwork, there were no problems, only the occasional fall out with my sister. Everything was fine until I slipped up and got caught in another case that resulted in me being sent back to custody.

Being adopted was no doubt the best thing that has ever happened to me. It has its ups and downs, and I would be lying if I said that there had not been times when I'd wished I hadn't been. Although my actions don't often show it, I'm grateful for what Mum and Dad did for us. Had it not been for them, things would have played out very differently for my sister and me. Over the last 13 years, they have continued to love, support and refuse to give up on us, despite everything that they've been put through. I hope that when I have my own children, I will be as good a parent to them as mine have been to me.

I'd like to say Rest in Peace to my Aunty Dawn and my mum X. I wish I'd been given a chance to see you, even for just two minutes. Even though I didn't know you that well, I still love you.

Finally, I'd like to say a huge thank you to Mum and Dad for everything. If it weren't for you, we wouldn't be here. I'll love you both forever. "You can't make a rainbow without a bit of rain."

## Jenny's perspective

I don't really like being called adopted even though my Mum and Dad aren't my real parents (meaning I wasn't born in my Mum's womb), I still see and class them as my Mum and Dad because they brought me and my brother up from a young age, and they will always be the Mum and Dad figure.

Since I came into my parents' care, I've never called them by their first names, always Mum and Dad. I have a good bond and relationship with my Mum, especially. I would say, my bond with her is stronger than the bond I have with my Dad, but I still love him. My brother and I are really thankful for what my Mum and Dad have done so far and continue to do for us.

For further reading, please see Appendix 1, which is an interview I had with our consultant psychotherapist, who had formerly worked for Social Care. In his interview he spoke frankly about the flaws in, what he calls, 'an under-resourced system.' He shares his view on what he believes could be done to support adoptive families.

It is a well-known fact that children and young people who have been in care are more likely to become involved in the criminal justice system. Although the statistics I've come across refer to children in Local Authority care, more than to children who are adopted, there are striking similarities between the two groups, in terms of the children's early experience of trauma and loss, and the lack of relevant mental health services available to them and their families.

# STEP 4—WALK THROUGH THE PROCESS

The social media world has created more distractions in our lives. We are bombarded with advertisements to purchase the latest gadget. But it doesn't always save time. Sometimes, it increases the time we're trying to save. Shortcuts aren't always the best choice.

I've found that lessons are learnt in life when we are unwilling to walk through the process. Opting out and giving up isn't the answer. Again, I asked for an instant miracle where everything would be over, and I could get on with 'business as usual'. Well, I hoped I would have made some changes, but perhaps it wouldn't have worked out as I planned. In any event, there were many miracles along the way that I didn't recognise, and at the same time, I discovered that God's purpose was to teach me patience and endurance. He revealed Himself to me at a deeper and higher level than I ever knew.

When things weren't working out for my children, I came to the conclusion they had to learn for themselves. Tony had been saying this for years, but I wanted to save my children from the mistakes they were making, repeatedly.

## Parenting children with complex needs

Learning about how our brains function is fascinating. According to Dr. Glaser, there is a lot of evidence to show that there are changes in brain function, which result from child abuse and neglect. Furthermore, she says:

*Hyperarousal, aggressive responses, dissociative reactions, difficulties with aspects of executive functions and educational underachievement thus begin to be better understood.* (Dr. D. Glaser n.d.)

It all made sense to learn that our brain develops in accordance with the way we are cared for in the womb and early childhood. We don't know to what degree they experienced substance abuse in the womb, but we do know the child following our daughter was severely disabled. When he was born, he spent a period in intensive care unit, due to the withdrawal symptoms he suffered from drugs while he was in the womb. Once again he would be separated from his mother for the rest of his life. Can you imagine yourself as a tiny infant completely dependent on your mother to keep you alive? Then you will get the idea of how being separated from her could feel life-threatening! After he was born, he was placed, by the local authority, in a home for children with disabilities.

The children wanted to see their brother, so we made the arrangements and went to see him. We knew of his difficulties and prepared the children for the visit. When we got there, he looked uncared for which was distressing to see. He didn't recognise his siblings, nor could he speak or walk, and was propped up with pillows in a wheelchair. Jason was the kind of child who would push to get things done. He was desperate to see his brother standing up. The worker organised for his brother to be strapped up in a body brace to help him accomplish this. We all gleefully applauded their brother who took small steps toward his siblings.

Despite how hard we tried to prepare the children, it was still heart breaking for them to see their brother that day. On the way home Jason thought it was a good idea if we brought their brother home and adopted him, but of course, it wouldn't have been possible. Years later, we learnt an older couple had fallen in love with him and were now caring for him. They had their home adapted to provide a better quality of care than he was having in the children's home and he is doing well.

The effects of traumatic early experiences inhibit our ability to form trusting relationships and develop healthy, well-functioning brains. Traumatic experience is defined as anything a child experiences as life threatening and includes the four forms of abuse (Dr. Glaser).

I remember feeling completely surprised when Eil described the size of a brain in children who experience trauma. It is half the size compared to children who have had a 'normal' start in life. I hadn't appreciated that the brain was still developing and continues to grow after birth. According to Dr. Glaser, the brain grows to the degree of 80-90 percent of its adult size in the first three years of life. This was an interesting piece of information that helped me to have even more understanding and compassion towards my children.

Setting and keeping boundaries were important strategies for our children. When they first arrived in care, they didn't know that night time was for sleeping and daytime was for doing normal activities. It was the other way round for them. Their brains had to re-learn and adapt to doing things differently.

Giving the children structure was an important way of bringing order and routine to their lives. At first they responded positively with the support we put in place for them. A few examples of the strategies we used are provided in Appendix 2. By the time they reached adolescence, however, we witnessed how much more difficulty they had with order and routine, and still needed the same level of support and nurturing. It all began to make more sense to know that:

*For a child developing in a high-stress environment, the regulatory abilities of the brain stem are already impaired at birth* (Dr. D. Glaser n.d.).

When children experience consistency in loving relationships and low-stress levels in early childhood, it actually builds their brains. It helps to equip them to learn, share, empathise and regulate their feelings. They are able to feel good about themselves and others, and are able to withstand everyday stresses (Adoption UK).

We noticed the difference when the children were calm. Their thinking and reasoning skills were more acute. When anxious or stressed, they could 'lose the plot' quickly. In reality, it was difficult to keep a calm environment around them all of the time. The children found it difficult to articulate what was going on for them when they had feelings of anger. They didn't know how to separate events happening outside our family home and tended to project the issues, like a fall out with friends, unto those who loved and cared for them. Of course, even adults behave in the same way.

They've come a long way, from punching the wall or smashing items in their bedrooms or whatever they could find, when they were angry. According to Adoption UK, the feeling of safety and security, in a calm environment, is a tremendous help for the brain to function better.

## Getting the right level of support

As our children approached teenage years, their behaviour was almost identical. Jenny fed off Jason's behaviour, but a new watershed moment arrived. We just didn't know who our daughter was becoming. It was totally out of character for her, and we weren't expecting this extremity in her behaviour. Finding friends similar to her was of paramount importance to Jenny. She was just like any other teenager, but there were some imbalances here.

When they gravitated towards the wrong crowd, we found it difficult to distinguish between the effects of their complex needs and what was typical teenager behaviour. Jenny got into scrapes with the law and the judicial system. She seemed to get excitement from her risk-taking behaviours. When she was in care, she got herself tattooed, while she was underage.

Social Care repeatedly used the same methods, even though they weren't working. Jenny was moved from one placement to another, but she continued running away and going missing.

Finally, Jenny was placed, by the courts, in a secure unit for girls, for her own protection and safety. Nothing else had worked. We continued visiting her regularly until she was returned to our care. Parental responsibility was shared with Social Care, and there were enormous repercussions. The children played one 'parent' against the other. But we stuck to our principles and values. Finally Social Care agreed to fund therapeutic treatment. Jenny co-operated while she was in the unit. However, shortly after she had returned home, they withdrew the funding.

The change of social workers contributed to the lack of continuity and the miscommunications that existed. It created more instability for our children who had emotional and consistency difficulties. The lack of resources and appropriate services has contributed to the unsettling periods in our children's lives.

Finally, Social Care accepted we were the best judge of our children, and qualified to know what was right for them. They had first-hand knowledge of our commitment towards Jenny and Jason and their reports became more positive and accurate. We went full circle and came back to the view that assessment and therapy were what was needed. Although they didn't verbalise it, in reality they knew that the lack of resources for appropriate, relevant services were the missing links.

## Useful tips

- Think ahead before you adopt. Make sure you know what God is saying to you about the situation

- Have prior discussions with professionals about the impact of the children's background and what it will mean when they are older. Don't be afraid to ask questions, even if they seem insignificant

- In most cases, children who have been in the care system will require some form of therapeutic intervention. Make sure the right therapy is part of the care package of support, even if it means sourcing from a private therapeutic service. Remember your own needs, in the package of support, in the longer term

- Don't be afraid to challenge and speak up. Parents are the best ones to know what their children's needs are and the level of support they require

- Think about the ongoing support you might need and ask for it

- Ensure there is commitment by professionals to longer term support and discuss regularly in review meetings

- It is important to ensure discussions and outcomes are documented accurately in the children's care plans

For more information on:

- Human Brain Mapping, please visit: http://onlinelibrary.wiley.com/doi/10.1002/hbm.21052/full

- Attention Deficit Hyperactivity Disorder (ADHD) Symptoms, please visit: http://www.uhs.uk/Conditions/Attention-deficit-hyperactivity-disorder/Pages/Symptoms.aspx

- Children with Special Educational Needs, please visit: https://www.gov.uk/children-with-special-educational-needs/special-educational-needs-support

# STEP 5—PLAY TO YOUR OWN STRENGTH

By now it was evident to the professionals we weren't giving up on our children. Our unconditional love and commitment were tested and stayed the course of time. The professionals had failed to work with the strength of our family. There were many occasions we came close to throwing in the towel, but Jason and Jenny were part of us. We held our faith in Jehovah El-Shaddai, the Almighty God. He gave the children to us. Our lives and resources were invested in them. We were their 'forever' family.

I remember earlier on, when school couldn't manage our son's behaviour, and owing to the child protection intervention, we were being blamed for his behaviour, to the point we felt unable to be open with the professionals. The psychotherapist supported us and agreed the children's risk-taking behaviours were linked to their past. They were emotionally damaged.

Social Care attributed the adoption breakdown to our parenting style, and offered to do parenting sessions. We co-operated with them, but soon the sessions fizzled out, primarily because of the numerous changes in social workers; they didn't have the staff, and there was much inexperience in the team. During this time of added pressure, I was still 'walking through' chemotherapy treatments.

At that time it was the same old story. Our views were being dismissed, because based on the children's level of intelligence and polite manner, and the brief time spent with them, the children came to be viewed as 'normal.' There was a reluctance to admit that Jenny and Jason had complex needs.

Neighbours witnessed the times when police came to our home. They couldn't understand how the children got into so much trouble, since they were so courteous towards them. They said it was to our credit, and that we should be proud of that.

## One size doesn't fit all

Finally, we made a formal complaint to senior managers of Social Care. The service we received had been sub-standard, bringing more tension to the family unit. Our complaint was eventually upheld. This was another period of anxiety and our stress levels were raised much higher than one can imagine. There didn't seem to be an end to it.

We raised around thirty complaints and most of them were upheld. A formal letter of apology was sent to us, together with an action plan. It set out a plan of how they would rectify the issues we had raised. The plan lacked commitment, and even though they set out objectives, there was no plan given on how this would be implemented and monitored. No one responded to this when we pointed it out.

They wanted us to accept the services they could afford, which were 'in-house' services. They fought us strongly on this issue offering services that were irrelevant to our family. We refused to compromise the belief we had held. Our needs were unique. We were honest and forthright. We were true to our convictions and planned to stay the course, however long it would take us.

> We were true to our convictions and planned to stay the course, however long it would take us.

Our dissatisfaction continued, and we escalated our case to the next level. The next stage of the process was to attend an independent panel meeting. We called on my family for support.

All of my sisters and my brother, Peter, attended the meeting. The level of their support was next to none. It meant everything to us. It was emotionally taxing, and an experience we wouldn't want another family to have to face. There were misinterpretations of what we had said and a lot of untruth that had been documented.

However, it gave us the opportunity to put the record straight. The panel agreed we had been failed and this was largely in the area of verbal and written communications, which was a major part of our complaint. They agreed that Social Care hadn't been fair about the therapy they had promised and, at the time, had failed to fulfil.

In time to come, we experienced changes towards us. An independent reviewing officer told us how impressed she was by the way we maintained our dignity. She also advised us to get legal advice.

For many years, Jenny and Jason were absolutely oblivious to what we were subjected to, but the time came when Jason started to show his appreciation for what we went through for them.

## Know your parental rights

My sisters were instrumental in their support of us over the years, but they had their individual concerns over my health. They too had seen from a distance the highs and lows of parenting our children, and this had impacted the extended family more than I had realised.

Eil made lots of enquiries on our behalf and signposted us to various organisations. We got involved with organisations such as Parent Partnership, Adoption UK, and Parents' Forum, to name but a few. We found out what our parental rights were, and felt empowered to continue our fight for the services our children deserved.

Parent Partnership made an educational film of me talking about my experience of school. It gave me a platform to speak about the negatives and positives of mainstream school. The film was used as a basis for discussion with a group of head teachers.

We were articulate and represented ourselves in a professional manner, but this became a stumbling block for us in many ways. Very often professionals viewed assertiveness with suspicion and in a negative light. They were not used to parents standing up and challenging them.

Father God opened doors into the best senior schools academically for our children, but they were in the minority. Jason was articulate and a gifted child, although it was overshadowed by his behavioural difficulties. Where there were inequalities in school we would challenge them. As a parent governor, I attended training for school governors. I was able to draw on the knowledge and expertise I had gained, in campaigning for the right services for our children. It transpired that some schools didn't have the right policies in place and, as a result, they were forced to update their policies.

Over the years, Father God placed the right people in our path, and we found invaluable help and support from friends, particularly our friend who was an experienced Guardian Ad Litem, and university lecturers who were former social workers. They understood the issues and were in agreement that we had been badly let down.

## Early intervention versus crisis management

After a long drawn out process of meetings, we came to the conclusion that we were the better judges of what was needed, but Social Care was unable to deliver it. Our needs were: to have the right therapy for the children; support to help to parent them from adolescence to responsible adults and periods of respite care.

When funding for therapy was agreed, several sessions were planned for the children and us. However, the managers of Social Care (formerly called Social Services) withdrew the funding, without giving any notice, and with little explanation.

Whenever the children's behaviour spiralled out of control, Social Care intervened with crisis intervention. At separate times the children were moved from one placement to another and further away from home. We travelled hundreds of miles to see them. In a sense, it moved them away from the wrong crowd they had mixed with, but on the other hand, it created more anxiety especially for Jason who was moved approximately twenty times. It was only the Grace of God that enabled us to keep going.

The 'Welfare of the child is paramount' became a legal principle in the Children Act 1989. It focussed on the protection of children by putting them at the centre and giving them a voice. While the children's wishes and feelings were important points to consider, they didn't have the maturity to decide on important decisions about their future. They needed the adults around them to take the lead. The time came when the children were given the choice to have therapy or not. On several occasions they opted out. They were used to making their own decisions and it caused clashes at home. When they left care, it became increasingly more difficult to manage this.

We have consistently held the view that education secures the future of young people, and were baffled when a social worker couldn't understand this. Had we not been persistent in this approach, our children would have left school without any qualifications.

The setbacks we experienced could have been avoided. As the children came from a different local authority, we were like a tennis ball, being passed from one authority to the other, over the issue of who would pay for the services that were needed. This became a bone of contention, and we were caught in the middle. The local authority would wait until we reached a crisis before they intervened. It was easier to blame us for the breakdown.

I'm all in favour of the government promoting for more families to foster and adopt children. At the same time, more money is needed to finance the resources that families will need in order to succeed. Once children are placed in families, it's as if everything will be normal. The families are then left alone to pick up the pieces when there are problems. There is a huge disparity between the budgets of local councils in different areas of the country: this shouldn't be the case. Monies should be ring-fenced for packages of care to support each family according to individual needs. This is a fairer approach. No parent should be left to fight for the funding they need. It is imperative that the education, care and judicial systems all work in unity to support children who, through no fault of their own, end up in the care system.

## Useful tips

When things have broken down, there's a tendency to remember the negatives more than the positives, regardless of how many positives there are. This was the experience we encountered with the people we turned to for help. I hope this checklist will help families and professionals to move forward.

- Establish and work with the family's strengths
- Find suitable training courses to help parents understand the emotional wellbeing and brain development of children as they grow older
- Ask your workers to send you on training courses to help you understand the child's racial heritage and the impact this may have on them and the family unit
- Train staff to provide relevant support for adoptive children in school
- Early intervention is more economical than waiting for the family to reach a crisis
- Social work staff should always keep in mind the Early Year's model

# STEP 6—BUILD ON A STRONG FOUNDATION

## Unconditional love

The Greek word *agape* means to love as God loves us, unconditionally. It is this kind of love that the Spirit of God deposits in our spirit man when we receive the new birth in Christ. It is this love, and only this love, that can endure eternity. In the Bible, the Apostle Paul describes this kind of love. It is one that *"endures long and is patient and kind. It can never fail or fade out or become obsolete or come to an end; it takes no account of the wrong done to it; it bears up under anything and everything that comes . . ." (I Corinthians 13:1-13).*

Naturally, we loved the children from the time we saw them; we didn't know how much our love would be tested. Marriages can break up from the least amount of tension, and certainly, our marriage was put under a lot of strain. Some of the professionals working with us were somewhat surprised at our coping strategies.

Our foundation was and is Father God. He took us through the storms of life and would take us through the journey ahead. There were indeed moments when we strove to make things happen by ourselves, but I now know the extent of God's mercies and grace that showed up through the prayers and support of family and friends. It's a true saying that *'love always finds a way.'*

We weren't only attracted to the children's physical beauty; we were filled with compassion towards them. No matter how we talked about the children's past, they were still judged by those who didn't understand.

We passed on our values to the children, and people were captivated by their friendliness and politeness.

The old adage that 'a picture is worth a thousand words' shows how a complex idea can be conveyed with just a single still image, and that image conveys its meaning or presence more effectively than a description can. When we saw our children in a photograph, our first impression, as they posed for the camera, was the way they laughed. Something or someone made them laugh. The camera captured this beautifully. The excitement on their faces was attractive. Jason has a mischievous grin. His hazel brown eyes told a story that he carried in his heart. I still see the sadness in his eyes.

There are aspects of people's lives that are hidden from others. Jenny had learnt to mask what was going on inside her calm and beautiful exterior. Our deepest fears and pain cannot be hidden from the Sovereign God, who sees us through His x-ray eyes.

I endured the shame I felt when the children got into trouble with the law. It was a major factor for me; we had never experienced that side of the law before. Fear is disguised as shame. A fear of what others think. Their behaviours put us in incriminating positions. We never supported the wrong they did, although amongst the speculation, people pointed fingers of accusation. They didn't know all the facts, and in any event, it wasn't as though their own children were perfect.

When police vehicles parked outside our house because of the children, I used to say '*Whatever will our neighbours think?*' Our house had been burgled before the children came, but when the police raided our home, it made us feel more vulnerable than the burglary did. We brought up the children to be law-abiding citizens, but when they got into the wrong company, they had to face the force of the law. There were instances when the police over reacted. When I complained, they usually opted out with the response: "How can we resolve the matter, Mrs. Fraser?"

The children knew right from wrong, and knew about the dangers of being in the wrong circle of friends. They were looking for their identities in the wrong places.

We live in an affluent neighbourhood. Our neighbours had seen the children growing up and had great admiration for the way they were raised, but on many occasions, they wondered why in the world we still carried on. Whenever I felt discouraged, my sisters reminded me to hold my head up as there was nothing to be ashamed of.

I smile as I remember examples of the children's impulsive and reckless behaviours. Even now I can't understand how in the world they had the nerve to do the things they did. Why on earth would you take your parent's car when you know you've never driven before? Added to this you were a minor. I wondered, 'Were they completely oblivious to the dangers involved?'

Growing up, I was protected from a lot of things and led a sheltered life. When I compared my sheltered upbringing with the 'exposure' of my children during their formative years, it was a steep learning curve for me.

To say it's frustrating that Jenny did not learn from her brother's mistakes is an understatement. Jenny followed in his footsteps, when it came to recklessness. I remember how she used to reprimand her brother; telling him about the 'dumb things' he did. They couldn't rationalise the reasons for their actions.

Attending court and police stations with the children became a regular feature but the time came when the stress of it all was too much. No matter how we lectured them, it just didn't seem to be going home. Finally, they got the message when we stopped going with them.

If you can think of the worst-case scenario that the average teenager has put their parents through, and multiply that a million times more, you will begin to understand our experiences.

Our Christian beliefs were viewed negatively by some professionals. Yet, they are the same principles which are fundamental to rearing children in stable homes.

If we didn't laugh at some of the things we went through, we would certainly be left crying all of the time. Our friends have told us we deserve a medal. Tony told me I deserve a 'Mother of the Year Award' for commitment, sacrifice, and dedication. This made us laugh together.

Although our Christian witness has taken us into darker places, I know that light is more effective in the darkness. Jesus calls us to be lights in dark places.

Jesus calls us to be lights in dark places.

At times, I wondered whether I was compromising my faith. Was I dishonouring God? Yet I knew we were trying to help two children whose past was catching up with them. I grappled with my conscience on many of these issues.

The level of stress had become unbearable and was coming from all angles. For too long I had been papering the cracks. The time came, when I questioned whether I was being fair to my husband, because I knew he no longer wanted this level of stress in his life. I watched how it affected him, and both our families. I questioned God on several occasions. Should I give up the fight? Was it a hopeless case? I struggled as I watched the children's reaction when they no longer received cards and presents for birthdays and Christmases, as they normally would. Jenny asked the reason why. She seemed oblivious her behaviour and the stress they caused were the main factors. There were many times when I missed my own mother, and wished she was still alive. I know she would have shown unconditional love for Jenny and Jason, the grandchildren she had never met.

## Going the extra mile

Our well-meaning family and friends have walked with us on our journey. They love the children but want us to put ourselves first and fulfil the dreams we have. Call it a sense of responsibility, commitment or just simply being a parent, but you don't give up on your children. They were a part of us emotionally—in our achievements, disappointments, and triumphs.

Now they are young adults, I've come to the realisation, they must learn from their own mistakes. I can no longer pick up the pieces and make it better. The greatest thing we can do for our children is to pray for them.

They have started to empathise and appreciate what we have done. It's a step in the right direction. Very often Jason will say, *'Mum why don't you and Dad go away on holiday. You deserve it'.*

When their birth mum passed away, Jenny, in particular, appeared unfeeling. When she saw how alarmed I looked, she asked me: "*Well how should I be feeling?*" I was surprised by her response. This was a genuine question as she didn't know her mum. It gave me the opportunity to speak about feelings and relationships. As the older child, Jason's attachment, particularly to his birth mum, was more significant. For him, it was like going back into a traumatic place again, especially as he wasn't given the opportunity to say goodbye to her.

The children's psychotherapist explained the importance of Jason and Jenny developing feelings of empathy for others. Jenny has started to express her feelings in writing, something she found difficult. Jason, on the other hand, has always been able to express his feelings in drawings, poetry and, more recently, his letters. I have begun to see feelings, values, beliefs, ideas, and behaviours evolving as they search for identity. The following messages are shared with their permission.

Jenny, aged 16 and 10 months, wrote in her Mother's Day Card 2016 to me:

> ". . . *Happy Mother's Day, Mum, you're the best. I'm not sure what I would do without you. So, thank you for all that you have done . . . Love you lots Mum even though I don't show it sometimes. You're only daughter.*"

It is said that 'absence makes the heart grow fonder.' Jason's message to me in one of my Mother's Day cards, reads:

> *No words can truly express how blessed I am to have you as my Mum. My angel, my hero, my best friend. Without your love and support over the years, I wouldn't be here today. I miss you lots and I know you've heard it more times than you've had hot dinners, but I really am sorry for all the times I've let you down. Thank you for always being there for me.*

For our 34th Wedding Anniversary Jenny wrote:

> *To the greatest Mum and Dad . . . I love you so much*

## Walk Side by Side

When the children were approaching teenage years, friends became an integral part of their lives, even more than family. They needed to maintain what they called, 'street cred', and referred to people they didn't even know as 'fam.'

One Sunday afternoon, Jenny approached me at the end of the church service. She asked if she could go home with a friend from church. As we hadn't arranged it beforehand, I felt pressurised and didn't want to agree. I was annoyed because I felt I was being hijacked into making a decision on the spur of the moment. This was something they often did when they wanted to get their own way. Her friend stood next to her and was listening to hear my response. The children were skilful at controlling me in this way. I told her to speak to her Dad and I would agree with whatever he decided. When she told me, her Dad had left it up to me, I gave in. I was unaware our conversation was in earshot of another mother. When I told her, *"You have to be one step ahead of these children,"* she replied, *"But sometimes you have to learn how to walk together."* This spoke volumes to me. It was ironic when Jason wrote a message that said:

> *Thank you for everything Mum. Thank you for walking with me when leaving me behind would have been easier*

Years later, the Lord spoke to me in several dreams. In one dream I was walking up a steep hill with the children. Jenny was on one side of my hip, and I held Jason by the hand as we walked together. They looked similar to the age when we adopted them. It was a long way up the hill. We couldn't see what was ahead of us but kept on walking. I knew then that I was carrying the burden for the children.

On another occasion I dreamt that Jason and I were in the back of a large minibus. There was no one else there and no one in the driver's seat. I assumed the vehicle had broken down because it was stationary. I called out for help, and people turned up and started pushing the vehicle. Father God was putting people in my reach to help. It was a way of getting my attention to receive the help He was sending.

Whenever I would give up, the words spoken by that mother: *"But sometimes you have to learn how to walk together,"* echoed in my heart. It was a confirmation when Tony said we just couldn't give up on them. Our children were our assignment. God's Grace was more than enough to meet every obstacle we faced.

## The Father heart of God

The Father heart of God is revealed in the story of the Prodigal Son. It demonstrated a forgiving father, whose character portrayed consistent love throughout the entire story. It personified a loving God, a father who was desperate to see his son return home, despite the way his son had dishonoured him. The son knew he wouldn't be entitled to the inheritance unless his father had died. After receiving the inheritance, the son left home. All the time the father looked out for his son with great expectation, believing his son would one day return home. This story epitomises God's patience, compassion, forgiveness, and the price He paid for the lost. It's the God kind of love that caused Jesus to make a sacrificial giving of Himself for the sins of the world; a love that causes me to aspire as a Mother.

I've kept all of my Mothers' Day and birthday cards from my children. They had given me a card with the following words:

*A Mother's Love*

*A mother's love is something that no one can explain*
*It is made of deep devotion and of a sacrifice and pain,*
*It is endless and unselfish, and enduring come what may*
*For nothing can destroy it or take that love away*
*It is patient and forgiving when all others are forsaking*
*And it never fails or falters even though the heart is breaking*
*It believes beyond believing when the world around condemns;*
*And it grows with all the beauty of the rarest, brightest gems,*

*It is far beyond defining,*
*It defies all explanation,*
*And it still remains a secret like the mysteries of creation*
*A many splendorous miracle man cannot understand*
*And another wondrous evidence of God's tender guiding hand*

Helen Steiner Rice

Just like a protective hen towards her young chicks, I have learnt how to keep my arms around my children in prayer. Psalms 91 is known as our circle of protection from all that is destructive and discriminative.

It's easier to learn from hindsight and afterwards wish we had acted differently. In an unplanned moment, everything happens spontaneously. This is when you make the best of where you are. The unknown can be a place of unplanned pauses. It is a place where we are taught how to simply trust, and it is here in a place of trust you learn that in the Father's eyes you are the most important of His creation, and He pays full attention to every detail. Your concerns become His.

There is excitement when all the pieces in the jigsaw come together, and the picture is complete. Things begin to take shape as the Father brings together every detail in a timely fashion. It only happens when you and I co-operate with His plans. It's all part of seeing the bigger picture.

## Notes for personal reflection

Is it possible to build strong family units in the 21st century? When we build a Godly family unit on Jesus our Rock, our building will be solid. The Bible teaches that "*Unless the* LORD *builds the house, those who build it labour in vain. Unless the Lord watches over the city, the watchman stays awake in vain.* (Psalms 127:1).

The word 'house' refers to all generations of families. As the Master Builder, God designed the family unit to be the foundation of our society. People are placed in families to provide unconditional love, care, and support of each other.

What can I do to support the disadvantaged, the marginalised, the lonely, the orphans and the widows in my vicinity or elsewhere?

_____
_____
_____
_____
_____
_____

How can I make a difference?

- To my family?
- In my neighbourhood?
- How do I share the love of God to others?

_____
_____
_____
_____
_____
_____
_____
_____
_____
_____
_____
_____
_____
_____
_____
_____
_____
_____
_____
_____

# STEP 7—OVERCOMING THE ODDS

*To everything there is a season, and a time to every purpose under the heaven* (Ecclesiastes 3:1). Seasons are periods in a year that are marked by specific weather conditions, temperatures and length of each day. Although each season is marked out separately on our calendars, sometimes they merge into each other. In one day, our weather can change into several different weather conditions. Similarly, Father God uses different seasons in our lives to teach us how to trust Him impeccably. Sometimes, there is a blend of joy and suffering, but we know the storm will pass over.

At one point, the journey grew darker and more challenging than I had ever experienced. I didn't know where or how it would all end. My faith in God was strong, yet there were uncertainties. My own mortality flashed across my mind, and I asked the Father what was His plan.

I thought about how I had lost my mother to breast cancer, six months after she was diagnosed. It had happened so quickly, and at the time I was still commuting to the hospital where I worked. When I had asked about genetic testing, my request was declined on the basis that no one else in the family had ever had breast cancer. Therefore, I didn't meet the criteria.

Four years later, I was given a life-threatening diagnosis several weeks before my 50th birthday.

Even though women are encouraged to do regular examinations, in my case, there was no evidence that there was any lump. The only symptom I had was the fatigue I felt, which I put down to my busy life. By then I had been working full-time and had no break in my service of 33 years in the NHS. Evening and weekends were also our busiest times in church.

One weekend, we were attending a regional convention in Sheffield. My doctor had sent me for a routine mammogram, and my appointment was the following Monday. The appointment kept going in my thoughts the whole time. Those who knew about the appointment were praying. I took courage in Eil's reassurances that no matter what I would face, she knew that all would be well.

Tony and I went for the results, at the hospital where I was working. The nurse practitioner carried out a physical examination. There was lots of prodding about, but they confirmed they couldn't find any breast lump. We followed the nurse into the waiting room where I saw a familiar face. It was one of my work colleagues. I was surprised and relieved to see a friendly face. There was some abnormality in her results, and she was awaiting the outcome.

We exchanged stories and learnt we were both registered at the same medical practice but had never bumped into each other. Although she was older than me, it was her first mammogram. She didn't understand why the General Practitioner (GP) had sent me a year earlier. Then it dawned on me that Father God had orchestrated everything so that I could be seen sooner rather than later. Thankfully, my friend's results were clear, but I was called to do a biopsy. It was painful when they inserted a long needle in the tender part of my breast.

A well-meaning nurse had muttered something about women's breasts just being cosmetic and that we didn't really need them. I was shocked and stared at her. Her remarks practically stunned me into silence. I thought about it. 'Did I just hear that right?'

Following the biopsy, we were called back. We were greeted by a short White male who introduced himself as my consultant. He showed us the X-rays they had taken. He was direct, insensitive and had an abrupt manner. He spoke as if I was a statistic. It sounded so impersonal. The news that I had cancer was debilitating. I was determined that fear wouldn't take over. Even though I was feeling anxious about the results, I stood in faith.

I was hopeful when he told me he could offer treatment. I expected it would be some kind of medication but didn't think, for one moment, it would be a mastectomy. How could that be a treatment I wondered? We were shocked. He explained the cancer was oestrogen receptive, which meant it was hormone related. Although the cancer was the size of a pea, they were concerned about the pre-cancerous cells forming around it.

I fell back into my seat shocked, with my husband saying, in disbelief, "It can't be." When we asked for a second opinion, I envisaged he would refer me to a different hospital out of the area. Instead, he immediately brought in another gynaecologist, who was a Black female surgeon. (He probably thought that was what I had meant, but that hadn't even crossed my mind. It wasn't what I was asking for). Pointing to the X-rays, she repeated the same message. From then, Ms. Davis became my consultant. She was very friendly and open in her manner.

The next steps towards surgery were discussed. During the operation, they planned to take further biopsies of tissues from my breast and the lymph nodes under my arms to check whether the cancer had spread.

She cautioned us that chemotherapy and radiotherapy were still a possibility following the mastectomy. It was difficult to hear that, but nothing was certain at this stage. It all depended on the result of the biopsy as to how things would progress. Sure enough, the appointment arrived quickly.

## Standing at a crossroad

I was at a crossroad. I have never felt as indecisive as I did at that moment. God seemed far away, but of course, that was never the case. Tony and I continued to pray for a word from the Lord. We believed for healing and didn't, at that time, understand that Jesus had *already* provided healing at the cross. As I sat on the side of my bed one morning, I felt as though I was in a fog and couldn't find my way out. In that moment, my life flashed before me. I was certainly not ready to make a life-changing decision. Life carried on around me. Everyone carried on with their normal activities.

I couldn't bring myself to confirm the appointment for surgery. The hospital had reserved a bed, but I ended up cancelling it. I didn't feel ready to lose a part of my body. Tony supported whatever decision I would make—whether it was to believe for a supernatural miracle or go ahead with surgery. At the time, I didn't consider that God could use the doctors to bring about my ultimate victory.

My sisters urged me to have the surgery. Finally, the hospital sent a specialist nurse to my home. She was worried that I might delay the surgery to my own detriment. She wasn't a believer and said that over the years she had seen too many Christian women put off the operation until it was too late. Due to my age, and the fact that we had young children, she urged me to have the surgery.

One day, I was led to go through a few old telephone numbers and came across a name and telephone number I'd never used before. It was the lady that owned the Christian bookshop, just down the road from where I lived. I contacted her and talked through my dilemma. She invited me down. I agreed to see her straight away.

One of the first things she told me was that I didn't have to accept the first option that was on the table. Her teenage son was diagnosed with leukaemia and was on conventional drugs. She believed chemotherapy had caused him to become weak and frail. She was convinced the disease had something to with his diet. After her own research, she learnt about taking out dairy products from her son's diet. The change was remarkable, so much so that his doctors told them to continue with it. She was radical, but it helped her son to become cancer free for a number of years. The medical team were amazed at his recovery.

When her son started university, he went back to eating processed foods. The cancer returned, and tragically he died. She was convinced it was due to his diet and lifestyle. She recommended that I go on the non-dairy diet, and gave me a bundle of literature and CDs to listen to. She even gave me a bag full of apricot kernels, to take with me, and practically begged me not to have any chemo-therapy treatment, because she had seen the effects of it first-hand.

I felt empowered to do my own research. I learnt from Cancer Research UK that breast cancer affects 1 in 8 women, and in 2013, 53,400 cases of women were diagnosed in the UK. (C. R. UK n.d.)

It felt as though I was carrying a time bomb in my body, which was ticking very quickly. I was selective in what I read, as certain information would play on my mind and it was easy to convince myself that the inevitable would happen.

## Investigating alternatives

My sister-in-law, who worked for many years as a senior nurse, had just left the NHS and started her new job in integrative medicine. She was reassuring and sent me literature, websites, and books to help with my research. This was the first time I came across integrative medicine. I believe that Father God orchestrated the timing of her new job. She also sent me a book entitled 'Your life in your hands' by Jane Plant. Jane was a professor who worked with my sister-in-law at the same clinic. I contacted Jane, and she advised me to change to a non-dairy diet. This was further confirmation that God had orchestrated the whole timing and put the right people in my path.

Jane survived cancer, a term I didn't like to use. I wasn't a survivor but an overcomer. She believed that there had to be a dietary trigger for the disease. As she continued her scientific investigations, she became convinced that she had discovered a causal link between dairy produce and breast cancer. Her research led her to visit China. She saw there were a significant number of women in the West with breast cancer compared to numbers in China. Women from the Western world had far more dairy in their diet compared to women in China. Her cancer returned on five occasions, and by this time it had spread all over her body. She was given a short time to live. She threw out virtually everything, which was dairy, from her cupboards and fridge. Having changed her diet, the medics had seen significant changes. Eventually, she fully recovered from the disease. At the time of her book it was some 15 years later.

It gave me fresh hope and insight. I was in no doubt that my life was in 'God's hands' and not my own. I learnt that the medical profession was there to guide and give advice, but I could make my own choice. There were other options other than pharmaceutical medicines that were available to treat cancers. I was convinced to leave out dairy products and immediately started to make some lifestyle changes.

My sister-in-law made an appointment to see the doctor at her practice. I was touched by the care and love she and her husband showed towards me. They travelled a long way to take me to their home. Jenny and Jason were very distressed about the fact that I was going away. As I was leaving, they cried and held onto me. We held hands together, and Tony prayed. There was a great sense of God's presence and peace.

I spent the night with them, and the following morning I went for the appointment. My sister-in-law was on duty that day. As I sat in the waiting area, it occurred to me that in the scheme of things we had no discussion about how I would pay for the consultation. At that precise moment, Bridget handed me a note. "Don't be worrying Cinth; we will sort something out." It was a 'God moment'!

The specialist spoke with a soft tone and this put me at ease. This was a contrast to the clinical manner in which the hospital doctors spoke. After he had examined me, I shared my faith that I believed for my miracle. When I talked about the importance of prayer, I was pleasantly surprised when he told me it was scientifically proven that people who prayed had a better prognosis. Live blood samples were taken and analysed. He said 'I'm not telling you not to have the surgery, but you're 99 percent cured already." I was pleased to hear that but 'why wasn't it 100 percent?' I thought. I used the supplements he prescribed to build my immune system, and they helped me through the surgery. He agreed going on a dairy free diet would help.

From that trip, I felt very reassured and more at peace, and I decided to have the surgery. I felt in my heart it was the right thing to do. It was important to know I had more than one option. Father God doesn't take away our free will. He works with our faith and where we are at. I developed my faith through the Word. Father God led me to read, particularly the Psalms. This is where He revealed His love for me.

People sent me healing scriptures and prayed for my healing. It was incredible how Father God gave us a Word each time Tony and I watched different Christian ministries on healing and nutrition. They were specific and timely messages. I learnt how to speak faith filled words each day as I declared the healing scriptures over my body, mind, and emotions. My faith in God moved to another level. The healing scriptures became food for my spirit man. My body was getting stronger and there were great changes to my health.

My sisters gave me healing CDs and DVDs. They encouraged me all the way through. Tony and the children were my rock. One of my church sisters took the time to type out a long list of verses from the Bible relating to health foods and healing. That really impressed me.

Over the years my sister Eileen has always been a tower of strength. Her words, "It is well, Cinth," continued to echo in my mind.

13 years ago Eil gave me a card with a picture of two small girls. The picture reminded us of the bond we share.

In the card, she wrote: "*We have come a long way together, as kids, and we still have some distance to go. Sis, the 'going through' is not always easy, but it's the best journey you will ever travel with God in front, and goodness and mercy following behind. When it gets really tough, there are*

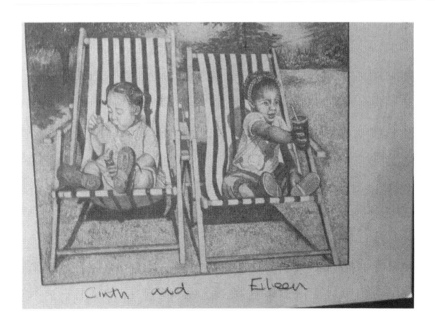

*only two footsteps in the sand, because, underneath are His everlasting arms. With all my love, Eileen and Verl."*

My bedroom became my place of solace. I found refuge in prayer. Prayer and intimacy with Father God was my first port of call.

Prayer and intimacy with Father God was my priority.

My husband provided nutritious meals. After our evening meal, I ran to my bedroom to pray. My children were about 6 and 8, and very often they would find me in the room praying. As I knelt at my bed, Jenny laid her head on my back, sucking two of her fingers as she usually did. Jason wriggled his way under my arms. It was a perfect picture of the Father in Psalms 91. It is a Psalms of protection and circle of His love, depicting an eagle with her young ones under her wings.

When I bathed myself in prayer, the Lord led me to read the Psalms—all 119 chapters. I was so blessed by them. It was as if I had never read them before. My heart was awakened to God even more. He equipped me for the journey ahead. I knew He would never leave me because He said it in His Word: *"Because he set his love on Me, therefore I will save him; I will set him (securely) on high, because he knows My name (confidently trusts and relies on Me, knowing I will never abandon him, no never"* (Psalms 91:14). I was ready for the surgery.

Tony's care and love for me went above and beyond. I watched as he cooked, cleaned, washed and ironed. He gave me my green juices every day. Our family benefited from eating more healthily, too. The non-dairy diet caused me to lose weight rapidly. I went down a couple of dress sizes. I felt well for the weight I'd lost; so much so that Tony gave me a new wardrobe of clothes.

I listened to lots of teachings and messages about God's love and begun a process of discovering God's love for me. 'He loves me. Yes, Jesus loves ME' I said repeatedly. I let it soak into my spirit and mind. He spoke into my deepest fears, as I had many. I understood that unforgiveness was rooted in fear and that God's love was the answer (perfect, developed love casts out all fears). I allowed Father God to heal me from all the hurt of the past, present, and future. I searched myself for any unforgiveness that could affect my relationship with Him. His unconditional love for me was not based on my performance—neither could I earn His love through good works.

In my search for a deeper path, my main concern was how I would get through this traumatic experience. I had neither time nor energy to analyse why it had happened. With hindsight, I came to realise that I had not yet learnt to rest in the finished work of Jesus through the cross: I had allowed the stresses and strains to take over my life. This was the major contributing factor. My journey now wasn't only about physical healing: it was a journey to *wellness* and *wholeness*.

I dared to venture into such a place of searching for more of God and the supernatural realm. As a believer, I was learning about who I was in Christ. I was hungry for the person of Jesus Christ and His Word. The Psalmist David wrote, "Taste and see that the Lord is good." I developed a love for His Word more than anything else. Whenever I had sad thoughts coming at me, I absorbed myself in reading and listening to His Word, and it diminished my fears and doubts, as long as I kept in His Word. Each day I took hold of the booklet written by Charles Capp, declaring the healing scriptures over me. It became my medicine. I declared my blood pressure was 120/80, and sure enough when the nurse examined me she said, "You have what we call a textbook reading. Your blood pressure is perfect."

God spoke in different ways. I believed His Word and was reassured that He would deliver me from the disease. I saw myself well and full of life. Prayers in my local church were offered for me. People sent prayer requests to different ministries around the world. I was immersed in prayers.

In a vision, the night before the operation, I saw myself lying on the bed in the hospital theatre. I was surrounded by the medical team. The Father and I were conversing. I sensed His presence at my side as we observed the operation together. The vision was confirmation that the operation would be successful. Father God had 'watched over His words to perform it' (Jeremiah 1:12).

Another one of my church sisters organised a prayer chain. She arranged for people to pray at hourly intervals from the moment I went into hospital until I was discharged to go home. She enlisted people from near and far to pray. On the way to theatre, I chatted and joked as the porters wheeled me down the corridor. Colleagues who knew me were stopping, surprised to see me, and wished me well.

Back on the ward, there was a real sense of camaraderie among the patients. They told me how long I was in theatre, and how long it was before I was out of the anaesthesia. They kept a watchful eye out for everyone on the ward.

I was on the ward for the next few days. Each day I became stronger and walked around without any pain. The nurses prepared me for the time when the bandages and stitches would be removed. When the day arrived, I followed the nurse into the treatment room. After removing the stitches, the nurse handed me a mirror and asked if I wanted to see my body. I had a quick glance at myself and almost fainted. It was a shock! I managed to stop myself from passing out. The nurse was impressed and remarked on how strong I was, but I didn't feel that way. It was all too difficult to accept a part of me was missing.

## Emotional and psychological impact

Physically, it didn't take me long to recover from surgery. I'd inherited genes that heal well. My surgeon had been extra vigilant with hygiene, and took the necessary precautions so that the wound would heal well.

Emotionally, I had learnt to be selective concerning those with whom I shared my diagnosis. I found that being around negative people was counterproductive to my recovery. They might mean well, but sometimes people want to gossip about other people's misfortunes. I wasn't about to give them the opportunity. I had to protect myself from the gossiping of others and withdrew from the people whom I found to be insincere.

The trauma to my body caused insomnia for a good twelve months. I tried anything and everything, but nothing worked. I was told that it was psychological, and was referred to a therapist. One of the questions she asked me was whether I had feelings of suicide. I made it very clear to her the thought never crossed my mind. I didn't go any further with the session, which incidentally, was over the phone. One of my nieces told me about the calming elements of juicing lettuce and celery. This was the missing link, and it worked.

At times, I wept for my loss. Emotional and psychological healing takes longer. It was in those times that Tony reassured me and told me he loved me just the same as he did before. I needed to hear that. So, I just got on with doing what I needed to do. I had to be strong for my children's sake.

I'm not sure how we approached the subject with the children. Jason was an avid reader and loved books. He came across a book I had inadvertently left out about cancer and the children found out what was wrong with their Mummy. They asked me many questions. From then on I was more open with the children.

There were many funny moments, too. Jason was an inquisitive child and found the prosthesis I kept in my wardrobe. Jenny told me how he paraded around with it under his tee-shirt. They were having fun.

Showering was the most difficult part for me. I didn't feel normal. My body was disfigured and I kept away from looking in the mirror without a bra. However, wearing the prosthesis gave me a sense of balance and confidence. I celebrated my 50th birthday with a new dress. I was thankful to God for the fact that I was alive and well.

I went back to work very quickly, but still I was 'walking through the journey' each day. There was light at the end of the tunnel as I waited the next few weeks for the results of the biopsy.

It was the most welcoming news I could have hoped for. When we followed the receptionist to the clinic room, Tony and I waited in silence. The atmosphere was tense, and my throat felt dry. I would like to have said that I waited in utmost faith and complete trust in God, but it felt more like waiting for an eternity—not knowing what the outcome would be. Even though I believed God's report, it still felt as though my life was in the hands of the clinicians.

I'll never forget the words spoken by my surgeon. She told me: "My colleagues and I were discussing your results together and I am happy to say there is no sign of any spreading of the disease, and you won't need chemotherapy treatment." A part of me had expected the good news, but it still took time to process what she had said. She looked for my reaction, and when nothing was forthcoming she rephrased her words "... well, I think this is something to be very pleased about ..." that's when I shouted jubilantly, echoing the words, "I told you that God wouldn't let me down." She replied, "Yes, someone up there is looking after you." This was the most welcoming news I had heard in a long while.

Now that the results were clear my reconstruction was arranged. My surgeons carried out a Latissimus Dorsi flap procedure, which took seven hours. I knew the plastic surgeon well as we had worked together some time ago. He was one of the nicest people I had ever met, and this was another God incident. They took tissues and muscles from my back to reconstruct my new breast. There was some setback in my recovery, as I experienced a 'wound breakdown.' This meant several trips to the hospital ward for dressing. They used different procedures that didn't work. My surgeon resorted to re-stitch some of the areas under local anaesthesia, a very painful experience. Still, the wound didn't heal, and plans were put in place for a further operation under general anaesthesia.

My daughter was so distraught at the prospect that I would go back into hospital. Jenny shouted out, "No! No more hospitals! It stops NOW." The wound soon healed, and sure enough there were no more hospitals, just as she spoke. It demonstrated to me the simplicity of having a childlike faith.

## Dèjá vu

In 2012, I received the news that I had ovarian cancer. This was a second diagnosis.

I had been visiting my local doctor for several months with symptoms of bloating in my abdomen and swelling in my right leg. Normally, I would stand in front of the class to teach my group. On this occasion, however, my right leg was very swollen and had to sit instead. There was a gynaecologist among the group, and during the break I spoke with her about the symptoms I was having. She empathised with me and agreed I should continue in my pursuit.

I was given all sorts of prescribed medication for indigestion and bloatedness. My GP had failed to link my current symptoms to the previous breast cancer diagnosis. I talked to Father God about it. That night I had the vision about water gushing out from my stomach. When I awoke from my sleep, I pondered over my dream as it was still unclear to me.

The following day after finishing work, I returned to Accident and Emergency. As this was my second visit, I didn't need another triage. Instead, an appointment was made for me to see the A&E consultant. It was a long wait, but eventually, he saw me. The next words he used were the exact words, describing what I saw in my dream. "You have water on your belly, but I don't know how it got there." I was amazed at how precise the message was. Enthusiastically, I nodded my head in agreement. At last, I knew what was wrong. He advised my GP to send me for a CT scan of the abdomen. My GP called and asked me to see her immediately. She gave me the news that it was cancer. I cried for a while in disbelief, and then dried my tears to face the journey. She was concerned about the fluid that had built up in my ankles and abdomen. I was admitted to hospital and stayed for one week while they carried out more investigations.

The doctors didn't want to drain the fluid (ascites) for fear of spreading cancer cells. Eventually, they made the decision to drain off the fluid. When the fluids stopped, the doctors arranged to remove the tube. But the tube appeared to be stuck. Several attempts were made by the nurses and doctors. You can image how painful it was. I screamed most of the time. Even Tony had to tell them to stop! The tube had somehow bonded itself deeply into my body. The only way, they told me they could remove it safely was to do a procedure in theatre. It was a very trying time.

The nurse brought me a theatre gown. As soon as I got up from the bed, the tube suddenly freed itself much to the surprise of everyone. Tony and I knew that it came out by God's intervention. It was as though He had said, "Enough, is enough!"

When we attended the gynaecology clinic, the surgeon introduced herself and told us that it was Stage III ovarian cancer and recommended I have a full hysterectomy.

This was a déjà vu moment: I had been here before. I agreed to the operation and stayed a week or so in hospital. This was followed by chemotherapy treatment and a further year of maintenance treatment. I didn't relish the idea of chemotherapy, but Father God graciously took me through the journey. Having had treatment intravenously for over a year, the main challenge for the nurses was finding my veins and inserting the needle. I spent the time praying every time they made an attempt to do it. I found the experience quite painful at times. Other times they got into my vein without any problems. However, I ended up with a port-a-cath inserted in the top of my chest, in order to complete the last months of treatment.

I was back to normal and was driving again within a short space of time. Thank God that once again, I soon received the all clear. I was undecided whether to return to work or not. I had considered taking early retirement before it all happened. It was coming up to a year since I was off sick from work. I had the opportunity to apply for ill health retirement, and my application was successful. I knew that God was positioning me for the next season of my life.

In 2015 I celebrated my 60th birthday on holiday with my family and siblings. We spent a week in Almeria, Costa Del Sol, and Barcelona. Leading up to the second week I became unwell. There were strange burning sensations in my body which I knew I had to investigate further. I was still an out-patient at the hospital. I had taken the time to check my symptoms out with my gynaecologist before we went away. He wasn't at all concerned, because he felt the symptoms were not focussed in one place, but I left feeling unsure.

Tony and I arranged to see the doctor in integrative medicine, on our return from Spain. We spent the night with his sister and family. The following day we saw the doctor at his practice. He was the one who took the matter seriously and told me there was something happening in my body.

I continued to see my GP over the next few months. The bloatedness and difficulty in digesting persisted. All the tests were coming back clear. Eventually, I was sent for an endoscopy because of the symptom of feeling the sensation that food was stuck in my oesophagus. A tiny camera was inserted through my mouth and into my abdomen. It was an unpleasant procedure. Thank God there was no evidence of upper gastrointestinal tract (GI) cancer, but there was indication of Dysphagia (difficulty with swallowing), a hiatus hernia, and a mild antral gastritis (inflammation of the stomach region). I was treated with antibiotics for the ulcer. However, given my medical history, the consultant followed her gut instinct and sent me for a further CT scan of the abdomen. They confirmed there was a recurrence of ovarian cancer, but surgery wasn't offered this time round. More chemotherapy was planned, instead. The same oncologist I had over the previous years, offered me more chemotherapy but warned me there would be no cure. It was at this point I was told that the symptoms were increasing, and I would have a few months to live. As difficult as it was to hear this news, I refused to accept her word on it. I told her that only God could cure me.

I had previously heard about Felicity Corbin-Wheeler through her programme, Get Well Stay Well on Christian TV and at the time my brother-in-law was ill. I arranged a telephone consultation. She strongly recommended contacting Oasis of Hope Christian Hospital (OOH) in Mexico (on the border of California, US). Felicity spoke highly of the Director and President, Dr. Francisco Contreras, MD. He had been her doctor when she was given the news of terminal cancer. She told me she owed her life to him. I hadn't heard of him before but felt the peace of God on the matter. From then onwards, everything happened rapidly. I checked out the web page she gave me about Oasis of Hope. I was unsure which route to take, as this time it would mean having to travel to another part of the world.

Here I was again, at a similar crossroad of my life. I had to decide whether I would go through the conventional or alternative route. All along Tony strongly believed we should go to Mexico. He didn't want to see me go through further chemotherapy treatment. I contacted Oasis and sent my medical notes to him. The secretary arranged a telephone consultation.

Dr. Contreras was extremely reassuring and told me that I was a good candidate for treatment. The survival cancer rates were of great interest to me. I found out they were three times higher than the national averages in the world. In contrast, I had been told, by conventional doctors, that there was no cure and I'd been given a few months to live. However, God's Word always has the final say. My confession was, "*With LONG life, I have satisfied you and shown you my salvation*" (Psalms 91:16).

We discussed these events with our families. I was even offered treatment by the doctor at my sister-in-law's practice. Added to everything else we considered, the fact that the Oasis of Hope had a Christian ethos was important to me and that swayed my decision. It was a huge step to take but I had the confidence that this was the right choice. I found their mission and philosophy statement about caring for the whole person, extremely supportive—

*First, do no harm (Inspired by the father of medicine, Hippocrates) and Love your patient as yourself (Inspired by the Great Physician & Healer—Jesus Christ).*

*These principles guarantee that our doctors will not prescribe any treatment that they would not take themselves or give to a loved one facing a similar diagnosis. Our focus is on the patient's quality of life; not just tumour destruction. We believe in the body's ability to heal itself when it is provided with the necessary resources, including immune boosting and anti-cancer nutrients, alternative cancer treatments, non-aggressive pharmaceuticals, healing foods and juices, emotional healing and spiritual care. The result is that most of our patients enjoy longer survival rates and a better quality of life than patients in conventional cancer treatment centres (Contreras 1997)[5]*

Father God knew how concerned we were about the side effects of pharmaceutical and conventional treatments. Tony had seen me go through that challenge before. It was a tall order, I thought, but we were at peace.

We didn't know how, but we knew the funds would come and sure enough, they did. God cannot fail when you believe. He works with the desires of our heart. We had further questions to ask Dr. Contreras, and when we spoke with him again, our concerns were alleviated. Our immediate challenge was finding £21K! I considered the online fundraising available for projects like ours but felt uneasy about that option. We prayed and believed God would provide the funds. Very quickly the funds were in place.

Our faith was stretched to new levels; more than I've ever known before. This was what God had shown me in a dream several months previously. I sensed the presence of the Father by my side. We began to converse and watched everything taking place from outside of a glass elevator. The elevator began to accelerate, moving higher and higher. I felt completely out of my comfort zone and shouted out something like: 'This is too much, I don't think I can go any further.' But it made no difference and I felt as though the journey was out of my control. All the time I knew Father God was close to me. Since that time I have looked over the past year of 2016 to 2017. The dream has become clearer. It was about a journey of faith and trust. My faith was accelerated to new levels.

> My faith was accelerated to new levels.

Our flights were booked, and the next day we flew to Mexico. It was like a whirlwind of events that were happening all at once. One minute I was discussing treatment in the UK and the next Father God had guided us to the other side of the world. The flight was eight hours one way and a new venture. Thank God, I was able to cope, even though I was very unwell. Oasis had made arrangements to meet us at the airport in California. Then there was the long drive across the border into Mexico.

Tony was protective of me. He was attentive and my literal rock. I couldn't have done it without him.

Oasis of Hope exceeded our expectations. The accommodation was hotel style. It was refreshing to be treated in a supportive manner as a whole person, rather than as a statistic. My treatment lasted for three weeks. I received high doses of Vitamin C, hyperthermia, and Dendritic Cell Vaccine. The on-site pastor led the daily devotions, which were uplifting. He went around praying for individual requests. A specialist medical team was on duty 24 hours. We found the education forums especially helpful and it gave opportunity for patients and family members to ask questions about their specific treatment and condition. The hospital had everything we needed and most of the facilities were on site. The meals and drinks were nutritious, and soon Tony and I were losing weight. We found everyone helpful and met some wonderful Christians from all over the world.

A Positron Emission Tomography (PET) scan was organised, and we travelled across the border to a hospital in California. This was the only facility Oasis didn't have. We brought the results back with us and saw Dr. Contreras with two of his senior doctors. They spoke frankly and honestly, but I wasn't as apprehensive as I had been back in the U.K. There were deposits of cancer in other areas of my body which he described as carcinoma. Their main concern was the 'large mass in my left abdomen, measuring 10.8 x 2.8 x 1.5 cm with a maximum SUV of 13.7.' But I was hopeful because of the first-class treatment I would receive. The treatment was rigorous. It was like condensing six months' treatment into three weeks. Soon the ascites (fluid) built up again, and my right leg became more swollen. They drained off fluid that made it easier for me. We received plans for follow-up treatment and bought six months' worth of vitamins and supplements. Soon we were on our flight home.

When the news came that my youngest sister was getting married and there would be another Tony in the family, we were all thrilled. Even walking was difficult, but I went with the rest of my sisters to help Rene find the right wedding gown. We knew they would be married abroad but didn't plan for it to be a 12 hour flight to Mauritius. I was asked to officiate in the proceedings and I toyed with the idea of travelling so far. My symptoms had increased. I wasn't sure if I could travel so soon after Mexico, but I was willing to make the sacrifice. It proved to be a test of my faith.

It was a precious moment to see my sister escorted down the aisle by our brother, Peter, and she looked radiant. That moment couldn't be captured from wedding photographs alone, I had to be there. Our new brother-in-law fitted into our family. I sensed our parents were watching and celebrating with us. The wedding was an amazing event and experience. It was picture perfect!

On our return from Mauritius, I was admitted to hospital following increased symptoms. I was very unwell with the ascites and mobility. The combination of long flights, travel and the ascites in my abdomen were contributory factors. On top of everything else I was going through, I developed deep vein thrombosis in the whole of my right leg. The oedema was significant. I had drainage from my abdomen before and after our trip to Mexico but the fluids had built up again. I wasn't at all mobile.

We arrived back in the UK. Following more drainage, I was transferred to one of the oncology wards. The hospital staff knew that I had been to Mexico so they isolated me as a matter of precaution. Everyone dressed in gowns and gloves, even my visitors, until all the tests were clear. I already knew there would be no threat to the staff or patients. Typically, the results didn't come back until I was ready to be discharged.

My oncologist visited me on the ward, and attempted to persuade me to agree to the chemotherapy treatment she offered. From the outset, she was against the idea of using the Oasis of Hope. Added to that she didn't support the Xeloda tables they offered, which was a significantly lower dosage of chemotherapy than orthodox treatments. Finally, she arranged for one of her colleagues to give us a second opinion. This didn't make any difference at all. He strongly advised against the use of integrative medicine. In his estimation, it didn't work, and he gave some random examples of a few case studies. To be honest, he knew very little, and could not, therefore, offer anything constructive. Unknown to my oncologist, her colleague who spoke with us revealed that using Xeloda was purely down to costs and had nothing to do with its usage. He told us it was very expensive.

We learnt from other patients who had also had treatment at Oasis of Hope. They told us Xeloda was available under the NHS in some parts of the country. However, my oncologist was not in agreement for its usage in ovarian cancer. At the end of the day, it all comes down to money and the patient's postcode.

We saw at first hand the tension between conventional and integrative medicine. My doctor at the Oasis of Hope hospital had been willing to speak with my consultant in the UK but she had refused. We found out from other patients that in their experience, there was scepticism amongst orthodox doctors. They felt there was still a small percentage, which were willing to work together for the good of the patient.

In his book entitled 'Health in the 21st Century', Dr. Contreras writes that doctors in Orthodox medicine are seeing a decline in patients, who had once trusted pharmaceutical medicine.

More people are finding out that they have the right to choose who they want to treat them. The pharmaceutical industry seems to be more interested in making money than it is about people's health. At the same time people are being supernaturally healed. Dr. Contreras has told us that he has seen miracles taken place in his practice. When believers release their faith in God, they experience supernatural manifestation in their bodies. I have read and heard many testimonies of the power of God working in people's lives that have helped my faith to be stronger. I am a personal testament to that. I know I am a miracle.

Ultimately, God is a healer, and all the glory belongs to Him. He has given the medical profession the knowledge, skill, and wisdom to promote life. I am thankful to the medical staffs who give their best for their patients. I have seen God work miraculously through the use of integrative medicine in my healing.

Following my initial treatment, the Oasis of Hope arranged follow-up treatments and telephone calls for as long as was needed. Owing to the fact that I was having Enoxaparin injections for Deep Vein Thrombosis (DVT), my doctors in Mexico informed me that Xeloda wouldn't work effectively with the injections, and I was advised to have the chemotherapy planned by my oncologist in the UK.

The side effects of chemotherapy were gruesome and challenging. Believe it or not but it was during this hard place I grew in understanding of God's love for me. He spoke through dreams and visions more than I have ever known. God's love for me was demonstrated through family and friends. Tony responded to my needs physically, emotionally and spiritually. On many occasions I had severe vomiting episodes. Tony was committed to carrying out the diet from Mexico. He did everything in his power to make sure I didn't lose my appetite and that I would gain more weight. I was more aware than before of how cancer affects the entire family and not just the person going through it. Even though Tony lovingly cared for me, there were times when I sensed it was too much, but he carried on.

Due to the side effects, my gynaecologist stopped treatment after four cycles of chemotherapy. Tinnitus was the result. The noises were pronounced to the point I had headaches. The ENT doctor referred me to the tinnitus clinic. The only help they could provide was ways of managing it. My oncologist began prescribing a drug called Lynparza Olaparib, which are chemotherapy tablets. For the best part I don't take pharmaceutical drugs, but in that instance, I have trusted the Lord's guidance.

## Loss and Separation

Grieving is universal, but unique and personal to each person in the way it is responded to. There is no right or wrong way to grieve. "Unresolved grief can lead to complications such as depression, anxiety, substance abuse, and health problems" (Melinda Smith 2017). It's a well-known fact that stress and anxiety are contributing factors that can trigger many illnesses and diseases in our bodies. They can have emotional and psychological as well as physical impact.

I looked forward to my sisters' visits, and when I became well, we would go out together. Their encouraging words, especially Eil's, gave me hope. By this time, she had nursed her husband through sickness. The passing of her husband brought Eil into a deeper place in her relationship with the Father than I have ever seen. I am truly amazed at how the Father takes us through those places of sadness, sorrow, pain, grief and brings us to a place of restoration.

Losing significant family members was traumatic but not because I didn't know where they were. On the contrary, they are truly walking in divine health now. Living in the presence of the Father is priceless and beyond our comprehension. Even though I am aware of this, it didn't stop me from feeling a sense that I was robbed. I felt it was much too soon. I miss them because they are no longer involved in our lives and share in our celebrations. I can no longer hear their voices nor have a conversation with my parents, especially Mum; my brother and brother-in-law.

I used to imagine the decision to take early retirement would bring a sense of elation. It was nothing like what I expected. I actually grieved over the loss of my career of 35 years. It was the social aspects and routines that I missed mostly.

As colleagues gathered at my farewell party, I gave my parting speech, 'There is life outside the NHS.' I had looked forward to a well-earned rest and to fulfil my God-given purpose. There were many staff members leaving the trust that year. Our 'golden hand-shake' for 35 years' service was only a small silver badge. It read 'Nottingham Hospitals 35 Years' Service. Somehow it didn't seem to equate to all those years I had given to the NHS.

My sense of loss was compounded by other events. I was impacted on so many levels. Eil suggested I get counselling. It wasn't automatically offered, but the hospital agreed to fund a few sessions for me. I was apprehensive about counselling, but my counsellor and I came to an agreement about how we would work together. It ended up that I actually looked forward to the sessions and felt sad when they came to an end.

Having finished work, I took time out to rest and reflect on the next stage of my life. It was then I decided to finish my book and start a new business. This gave me hope and optimism.

# STEP 8—ABIDE IN HIS PRESENCE

There is a secret place where we can feel safe and secure. To dwell is to live in that place. It is a place of solitude; a place of enrichment. We find security, comfort, refuge, fortress and deliverance from all evil. The Bible was written in Aramaic and translated into Hebrew and Greek. The Jewish nation had many names for God. One of them is El Elyon, which means the Most High. The other, El Shaddai, means the Almighty. *"He who dwells in the secret place of the Most High shall abide under the shadow of the Almighty"* (Psalms 91:1).

## Prosperity is the Father's Will

One of the ways God manifests Himself in the earth, is through signs and wonders. He works through and in us. There was a lot for me to understand of how to operate, rule and reign in the Kingdom here on earth. As heir and joint heirs with Jesus in the Kingdom, I gradually learnt about spiritual laws and how to exercise the authority I have as a believer.

Although I was born again, I didn't know that prosperity was a part of my Salvation. The word prosperity wasn't used much in some churches. Our church culture didn't teach that healing belonged to us; neither did we see much healing taking place in our congregations. We knew about being saved, sanctified and even tarried (waited) to receive the Holy Spirit. Tarrying suggested we were striving to receive what God had already freely given in Jesus. It was many years later that I found out there was a better way to live.

When Jesus said the words 'It is finished, man's redemption is complete,' it meant that I ALREADY possessed all of the Blessing in my recreated spirit. This included the fruit of the Spirit, healing and wholeness. God really wanted me well and whole and 'to prosper even as my soul prospers'. To prosper is to increase in every area of life including finance. In the scriptures, I read where Jesus healed them ALL.

> Jesus healed them ALL.

Putting our faith in the finished works of the cross is the only way to activate what God has already done.

The book of Ephesians tells how in Christ we have every spiritual blessing. All the blessings of God were already in Christ before the foundation of the world: our part is to receive it and take it by faith.

When we take the Holy Communion, it is a way of giving thanks for what has already been accomplished. Our part is to receive what is already provided. This revelation brought a whole new perspective to me. When you renew your mind to the Word of God, you too can receive this truth, and accept all that the Father has provided for us.

## Speak words of faith

I remember a particular occasion when I was healed supernaturally, without medication or intervention from the doctors. Many years ago, I was diagnosed with a suspected underactive thyroid. My symptoms were feeling tired and lethargic. As I was still working at the hospital in Mansfield, I went to see one our doctors, who carried out a blood test. The test indicated an underactive thyroid. He wanted to treat my condition with iodine but I asked if he could delay my treatment because I believed in healing and trusted in God. The doctor was surprised, commenting that he had never received such a request before but he agreed to repeat the blood test. He told me that he wouldn't be doing his job well if he didn't treat my condition; however, he repeated the blood test at my request. I remember the nurse in the room, at the time, looked somewhat bemused. He did this on two occasions.

When I returned for the results, he looked happy about the news he was about to give me. The results returned negative; it was a miraculous healing. He told me how he didn't expect this result and agreed something amazing had happened. Since then I have had no further issues, and that was some thirty years ago.

Speaking what God says through His Word is crucial to our healing. I was used to thinking things through, intellectually, but now I have learnt that all Jesus has provided comes by grace through faith. To believe in your heart (recreated spirit) and confess the words that God says is how faith works.

The old adage that 'sticks and stones may break my bones, but words can never hurt me' is indeed a delusion. *"And the tongue is [in a sense] a fire, the very world of injustice and unrighteousness; the tongue is set among our members as that which contaminates the entire body, and sets on fire the course of our life [the cycle of man's existence], and is itself set on fire by hell (Gehenna)"* (James 8:6).

It's far easier to say what your physical body is feeling rather than to say what God's Word says. It's a good idea to start speaking God's Word over your situation, no matter how you may be feeling. One of my favourite scriptures is:

> *But He was wounded for our transgressions, He was crushed for our wickedness [our sin, our injustice, our wrongdoing]; The punishment [required] for our well-being fell on Him, And by His stripes (wounds) we are healed* (Isaiah 53:5).

The battle takes place in our mind; whether to believe what God says about us or the lies and condemnation from the evil one. There were many times when I heard the words 'You're not healed! You're not good enough! Not everyone gets healed! You're going to die!' When our minds are renewed on a daily basis, our inward man is strengthened, and our thought patterns eventually change.

> *... and be continually renewed in the spirit of your mind [having a fresh, untarnished mental and spiritual attitude], ²⁴ and put on the new self [the regenerated and renewed nature], created in God's image, [godlike] in the righteousness and holiness of the truth [living in a way that expresses to God your gratitude for your salvation]* (Ephesians 4:23-24).

Just as there are natural laws, that govern our existence on earth, there are also spiritual laws that govern the spiritual realm. One of them is faith. God has given to every believer the same measure of faith. Essentially, it is God's kind of faith or the faith of God. It is our *spiritual* faith and not our *natural* faith. When we put the Word of God into our spirit being, we are one with the Holy Spirit, and faith comes. *"So faith comes from hearing [what is told], and what is heard comes by the [preaching of the] message concerning Christ"* (Romans 10:17).

Faith is trusting in God's ability. The Word of God has power to change lives. Since 2005, I have been taking God's word as medicine. Yes, literally. The Word is supernatural and not just a physical book with stories we read. The Word is alive and active.

> *My son, pay attention to my words and be willing to learn; Open your ears to my sayings. Do not let them escape from your sight; Keep them in the centre of your heart. For they are life to those who find them, and healing and health to all their flesh"* (Proverbs 4:20-24).

You can take this supernatural medicine without any harmful side effects. I shared this truth, about taking the Word of God as medicine, with a senior minister in one of our churches. "Sounds like you take the Bible literally," he told me. "I've never heard this before," he exclaimed.

In fact, the more you take it, the more your faith grows. I found all of the healing scriptures and other scriptures that the Lord led me to and regularly spoke them over my body and my situation. The Charles Capp book, I previously mentioned, was also instrumental to my healing. The words were powerful. There are numerous examples of how God's Word has worked in my life. I refer to these as 'God Moments'.

Faith breaks all the rules. When you are told there is no cure; it specialises in the impossible. I found out that I have authority over all the power of the enemy; over sicknesses, diseases, lack and torment—all of the curses. There are many examples of Jesus taking authority: He spoke to the fig tree and to the storm, and they obeyed Him!

The investment in intimacy with the Father reaps great dividends. It comes through personal devotions and quiet times reading, meditating on His Word, worshipping and listening to the Holy Spirit.

Jesus spent His earthly ministry preaching and demonstrating the Kingdom with miracles, signs and wonders. Over the years, I have learnt from many teachers in the Body of Christ, who have evidently spent time with God. Having listened to teachers from all over the world, I have learnt how to practice being in His presence. Father God has revealed Himself powerfully to me through His Word.

## Thanksgiving

I take my healing, at the same time as I make my request to God. This is what Jesus said, when you pray according to His will, believe, and you will have it (1 John 1:15). Healing is the will of God and He provided it through His body on the cross at Calvary.

When I went to the hospital (for my regular check-ups) after the final diagnosis of ovarian cancer, I received some fantastic news and I started to praise God. Immediately, I felt the Lord saying, "Did you have to wait to hear your results before you believed me?" This stopped me in my tracks. To this day, I continue to keep those words in my heart as a reminder: giving thanks is where the victory is.

The Lord revealed this truth to me in a dream. There was a knock on the front door and my daughter answered it. I heard someone saying, "Mrs. Fraser?" I came to the door when she called me. Standing there was a stern, looking man. I asked if I could help. He simply repeated what he had said before: "Mrs. Fraser?" and handed me an ancient looking tambourine. To my surprise, there was only one small cymbal on it. Nothing more was said. I pondered over the dream and asked the Lord what it meant. Was this the state of my praise? Had my worship worn out? I wondered.

From then on, I began to worship the Father, praising Him with the Psalms and worship songs. I still wake up in the mornings with songs of praise on my heart, and I take the time to worship Him. The key to receiving your healing, is giving thanks even before you see the manifestation.

Jesus is a faithful High Priest over our professions and able to bring to pass whatever we say according to His will. In the Old Testament, one of the responsibilities of the Levitical high priest was to make yearly intercessions for the sins of the people. Imagine having to wait a whole year to have your sins atoned for! Thank God, His sacrifice was once and for all, and He is forever present with us, at the right hand of the Father, interceding on our behalf.

## Useful tips

- You take the Word of God by speaking healing scriptures over your spirit, mind and body. Confess that Jesus is Lord over every area of your life. We confess or declare from the position that God loves us and we belong to Him. We can then speak faith-filled words, rather than words that come from a place of doubt or unbelief.

- When we profess God's promises over our lives and our bodies, our High Priest, Jesus Christ the anointed One, stands with us to bring His Word to pass. When we don't know how to pray, He continues to make intercession for us, and the Holy Spirit offers up our prayers on our behalf.

### *Action*

- Find the promises of God in the Bible concerning healing or any other needs and desires you may have. God, the Holy Spirit, is our Comforter. In the Greek the word Comforter has several meanings: Counsellor, Strengthener, Advocate, Intercessor, and Standby. Allow Him to lead you to the promises He has specifically for you. There is no magic formula: the Holy Spirit will manifest Himself personally to you. The experiences of how God works will differ from one person to another. Always listen to what the Holy Spirit is saying to you as an individual.

- Hold on to those scriptures, through prayer and meditation. Come in agreement with the Word. Consistency is the key to your victory. See yourself healed and whole and begin thanking Him for His provision.

- Create an environment of worship in hymns, songs and praise. Speaking in tongues is also used for prayer and worship. When we speak in tongues, in our devotions, we speak the mysteries of God.

- Take Holy Communion, as if you are confident that the redemptive work of the cross has been done, finished and complete, already. You have the promises of God RIGHT NOW in your spirit being. Release your faith in the finished works of Jesus and take your healing. Believe that God is working on your behalf in the spiritual realm. The Father commands the angels, who are ministering spirits of God, to move in your direction (Psalms 91).

- Faith works by love. Your faith is activated when you love. Forgive yourself and others as God forgives you, even when people don't admit they have wronged you. Don't hold on to grudges or ill feelings. These feelings will hold you back from receiving God's promises.

## Say

- I am redeemed from the curse of the law. Sickness and disease have no power over me. I am set free. I am dead to sin and alive to God. By His stripes I am healed and made whole

- No weapons formed against me shall prosper. Every tongue that rises up against me, I declare to be in the wrong. This peace (triumph over evil) is my inheritance as a servant of the Lord.

You can use other healing scriptures as you are led by the Holy Spirit.

# STEP 9—HAVE A SENSE OF ADVENTURE

Have you ever been somewhere for the first time, and felt the excitement and trepidation of being in an unfamiliar place? Does the feeling of uncertainty cause you to feel out of your depth because you don't know how things will pan out? That's exactly the place where God wanted me. I was so used to intellectualising everything in my life. I could easily plan out routes, itineraries, seminars, training programmes, etc. I did this for many years.

Journeys can be long and arduous with many rough terrains. At times we must bare all (strip right down) to God, because where He wants to take us to requires complete trust in His ability.

The unfamiliar and unplanned experience gave me a sense of adventure. When I looked for Him in a familiar place or a way I was used to, He would surprise me. I never knew how God would come through for me.

There were times when I had faith and doubt both at the same time. Is it possible I wondered? In Mark 5, when Jairus came running to Jesus' feet, begging him to heal his daughter, Jesus didn't condemn him. He reassured Jairus and spoke the words, "Only believe."

God has a sense of adventure. He takes us on paths with twists and turns. When you least expect it, He does something spectacular and innovative that transforms your thinking and the world around you.

Now, I actually look forward to see the way He will manifest Himself to me. When we confidently put ourselves in His hands, our victory is guaranteed. Trusting was an issue for me, but Father gave me His Word on it: *"Trust in and rely confidently on the LORD with all your heart and do not rely on your own insight or understanding"* (Proverbs 3:5).

## Miracles and 'God moments'

'God moments', along the journey, were the most precious and awesome times of my life: times when God showed up in unexpected ways. They are what I call the 'SUDDENLIES' of God.

The scriptures are filled with sudden moments when the Father steps in, because you have come to the end of yourself, and there is no other option.

When you consistently stay in the Word, and believe the promises of God, He will manifest Himself in ways that are beyond your highest imaginations and petitions. Christ is the Word, and we get the privilege of having Him take His abode in us. Jesus said, "*Remain in Me, and I [will remain] in you*" (John 15:4). Can you imagine that God the Father, God the Son and God the Holy Spirit lives in our recreated spirit?

There have been numerous miracles and 'God moments' where I have witnessed the out workings of the Holy Spirit. Meal times were an integral part of our family life. We sat at the table, together, eating and conversing. One day I had finished eating and, as normal, had retreated eagerly to my bedroom, to commune and worship with the Father, I heard Jason shout. "Mummy! Quick! Look through the back window!" I ran into Jenny's room and saw something amazing. There was a large rainbow—I believe it was a double rainbow. The colours were significantly bright. They were the largest and brightest rainbows I had ever seen. Knowing what it meant, Jason reminded me, "Mummy, remember God's promises." I was so blessed at this. I knew God was speaking to me through Jason. The peace I received was priceless.

When I was recovering from my first surgery back in 2005, Jason was about seven years' old. The children's hearts were so open to the Father. It was a defining moment to see how God used them to minister to me in different ways.

Each day I used God's Word as my medicine and professed His healing promises over each area of my body. Very soon the healing scriptures flowed out of my spirit as I spoke them, and I knew healing was taking place in my body.

Following the final diagnosis, I knew I had to make permanent changes, and decided to take a sabbatical from my ministerial duties.

I wanted healing but how much did I really know the Healer and Developer of my faith? I wanted to know what His plans were for my life. He revealed Himself in a two-fold vision.

In the first part of the vision, I saw a friend who was sitting in a hospital bed. There were two other people (whom I knew) in the room with us. I held a notebook in my hand as if I was taking notes for some kind of event. My friend was wearing a hospital gown. I was surprised at how well she looked as she had already died. When the others left the room, I stayed with her. She got out of the bed and I followed her as she went downstairs, into what looked like a basement, where there was a small office. In the office, stood a tall porter, who greeted her, and they spoke for a while. I recognised the porter from a previous employment many years before, and this resonated with me. I couldn't hear what they were saying and I watched as she left the room; went up the stairs and vanished out of sight.

The next part of the vision was significant. I remained in the basement, where I became aware of a presence beside me. There was just the two of us. He was a very distinguished looking gentleman with a warm smile. His presence was comforting and he seemed caring. I was captivated by the brightly coloured, tweed jacket he wore. The colours glowed. I knew this could have been the Father, Jesus or the Holy Spirit. He was elderly with white silver looking hair. In front of me, on the ground, were boxes full of index cards.

I was struck by the fact that it was a very old filing system, something I used when I first started working. I attributed this to something that represented the past. I carefully went through the boxes, which were sectioned off by the index cards. He didn't speak, but I felt a sense of calmness around him. He seemed confident that I wouldn't find anything. To my surprise I didn't find what I was looking for and started the process over again. He knew that what I was looking for didn't exist, but he watched as I searched again. This was the end of the vision.

The times where I have experienced the most growth in my life, were when I didn't know about something and had to ask my Father about it. On this occasion, that's exactly what I did because I wanted to know what the dream had meant.

A few weeks later, I started my sabbatical on a Sunday morning. Tony had left for church. When I got my Bible out and began to read it, I expected God to speak to me. As I read the Psalms, the Holy Spirit led me to several other scriptures and then directed me to Psalms 37:10. The Amplified Bible is my favourite translation. Psalms 37:10 read, *"For a little while, and the evil doers will be no more; though you look with care where they used to be, they will not be found."* That was exactly as I had seen in the vision I had. I was elated and stunned at the same time. I knew Father God confirmed that all of the enemies who were working against my health would be no more; completely eradicated; gone!

My oncologist in Mexico sent me for a PET scan. A PET scan is an imaging test that allows doctors to check for diseases in the entire body. The test took place on 15th June 2016 in California, USA.

I knew that God had given us the authority and power to *'Bind (forbid) on earth what has been bound in heaven, and whatever we lose (permit) on earth shall have already been loosed in heaven'* (Mathew 18:18). I started the process of binding each symptom in the name of Jesus, and 'loosing' the healing power of God over me. Some symptoms were the result of chemotherapy treatment. I kept a journal of the different physical and emotional symptoms I experienced in my body. Each time I had a victory, I would cross off the symptom, giving thanks for healing in those areas.

Six months later, my oncologist, in the UK, sent me for a CT scan on 5th December, 2016. This type of scan uses X-rays to make detailed pictures of parts of the body and the structures inside the body. When I enquired about having a PET scan, the hospital informed me that CT scans were normal standards of care for patients in the part of the country where I live. When the results of the CT scan came back they revealed that the sizes of the tumours in my stomach were substantially reduced. All my organs were now normal.

My doctors in Mexico and the UK were all very pleased with the report (see CT scan on the opposite page). This was indeed the hand of the Master Healer.

Another 'God moment' was the time of my sister's wedding in July 2016, when we went to Mauritius. I spent most of my time

**FRASER. HYACINTH E U**

Ref. Locn. : **MAIN OUTPATIENTS**
Referrer :

DoB :
Hosp. No. :
CRIS No. :
NHS No.

**VERIFIED**    Verified By : DR                     05-Dec-2016
    and : DR
    Typed By : EXTERNAL    05-Dec-2016

This is a FINAL report.

CT Chest/Abdo/Pelvis With Contrast  05-Dec-2016
Accession No: RX1901372848

Clinical Information: recurrent ovarian caner, struggling with chemo toxicity. good clinical response.. ? radilogical? patient wants to stop chemo,,;

Report:
Examination of chest, abdomen and pelvis with intravenous contrast.  Comparison is made with previous study from March 2016.

Left mastectomy with implant in situ.
No axillary or mediastinal lymphadenopathy. The lungs remain clear.

Normal liver, gallbladder, pancreas, spleen, kidneys and adrenals.

Within the pelvis there is a normal urinary bladder. There is a trace of free pelvic fluid and some soft tissue thickening in the presacral region, this is longstanding.

Previously visualised bilateral pelvic sidewall lymphadenopathy has significantly decreased in bulk.

No bone lesion.

Conclusion: Good partial response with significant decrease in bulk of pelvic sidewall lymphadenopathy.  No new adverse feature

Event Number :  E-901178209
  Ref. Source :  i

Examination Date :  **05-Dec-2016**

Nottingham University Hospitals NHS Trust - City Campus, NOTTINGHAM CITY HOSPITAL, HUCKNALL ROAD, NOTTINGHAM, NG5 1PB

  Examinations :  **CT Thorax abdomen pelvis with contrast**

in the hotel room because I was vomiting and fluids had built up. One day, Eil came to pray with me in my hotel room. We prayed and worshipped. The Holy Spirit came into our midst and gave a Rhema Word: a vision through Eil. As I looked up, I saw my sister radiating in brightly coloured clothes of red and gold. Eil told me, "Take your healing Cinth." Enthusiastically, I said, "Yes, I receive it." I saw her hand reaching out towards me. I stretched out my hand to take my healing. As I did, I found that my hand went through hers like an invisible glove.

When we returned to the UK, I still pondered over this for some time. As I searched for insight, the Father revealed to me that the supernatural realm is greater than the physical realm.

> The supernatural realm is greater than the physical realm.

He showed me that my spirit man was many times greater than my natural (physical) man. Your spirit being is the real YOU. I already possessed everything I needed in the spiritual realm. I made a note that my healing had taken place, that day, in the hotel room.

## Opportunities to reach out to others

Experiencing the NHS at first hand was an eye opener for me. I had concerns about the lack of information around the role of nutrition, diet and lifestyle choices, which might enable patients to improve their quality of life. It saddened me when I saw the lack of professionalism and compassionate care towards patients who were diagnosed with cancer. There are good, hard working and caring medical staff, but all wasn't well.

I have a passion about helping people, especially, those who suffer from cancer. We can help ourselves to prevent or combat cancer. One of our defence mechanisms against cancer is having a strong immune system. According to Francisco Contreras, MD (my Mexican consultant), our bodies rely on natural barriers such as the skin, nasal hair, mucous secretions, and inflammatory processes, but the immune system is our greatest defence mechanism. What is known by the medical profession is that chemotherapy and pharmaceutical drugs weaken the immune system. When this happens patients become more susceptible to infections. Both healthy and diseased cells are destroyed in the process (Contreras 1997).

On my trips to the chemotherapy suite, I would observe patients consuming packets of crisps and sugary drinks while they are hooked up to the IV machines. All around the hospital were vending machines with food items filled with inordinate amounts of sugar and salt. Why were these detriments to recovery and good health being ignored?

Making changes to improve and build our immune system is a shared responsibility with those who grow and supply our food as well as the consumer. We also rely on doctors and nutritionists to give us the right advice and help.

My treatment plan was designed by Dr. Francisco Contreras. Over three weeks in Mexico, I received high dosage of vitamins and supplements intravenously. The dendritic cell vaccine and hyperthermia treatments played a major part in building my immune system to fight off attacks from micro-organisms and toxins that enter the body. It helped me to recover well from chemotherapy. I continue to see the benefits of the organic foods I eat and the supplements I take. Having good hygiene is important to prevent infections. I was more aware of the importance of carrying a bottle of antibacterial hand wash with me.

I am ecstatic when patients ask me about food and nutrition. It is a great opportunity to share what I know and what worked for me. One lady asked me if I was a doctor. I told her that my research had revolutionised my thinking and I had been motivated to put what I'd learned into practice. Patients are either misinformed or ignorant about what they are consuming. A medical consultant told me, the advice he gives to patients was simply to have a balanced and healthy diet. When I challenged him on what he would describe as a balanced diet, he couldn't tell me.

On the chemotherapy suite, there was a volunteer worker, who went around offering sweets to the patients. When she offered me the sweets, I politely refused them. Naturally, she asked for an explanation. What another great opportunity it was for me to educate others!

God opened many doors of opportunities for me to share some of the things I had gleaned from the Bible; things I researched and my experience of integrative medicine. I was surprised by the number of people who were not privy to this kind of information.

I'm a conduit for helping people to make lifestyle changes. The saying is true that information is power but information isn't power until it's acted on.

There are great benefits of juicing organic green vegetables. Some of what I've learnt is shared in my recipes in Appendix 3. Avoiding sugars and certain sweeteners is crucial for people who have cancer, because it thrives on sugar. There are sugars even in natural fruits that should be avoided. I was surprised when I found out that some of my favourite exotic fruits from the Caribbean, like mangoes, pineapple, grapes and even bananas had significant sugar content. The good news is that there are alternatives that can be used, such as organic honey, Xylitol (which is a natural sweetener called sugar alcohol). Stevia is extracted from the leaves of the plant itself, and is also good alternative to sugar.

One day I had just finished a cycle of chemotherapy, and Tony had gone to pick up the car. While I waited for him, I began to feel unwell and very weak. Another lady was also waiting for her lift. She looked my way, and I remember thinking, I hope she doesn't want to have a conversation because I just didn't want to speak. She caught my attention, and before I knew it, we started to converse. Somehow I found an inner strength. The lady began pouring out her heart to me. Even though I wasn't feeling up to having a conversation, she carried on nonetheless. She told me how her husband had left her at the time she needed him the most. She looked frail and I sensed that she needed to talk to someone. I was the person. As her story unfolded, she told me she had been given a short time to live. I wanted to give her hope, in what looked like a hopeless situation. I told her that Jesus loved her. She found it fascinating and listened intently, hanging on to every word I spoke. When her son returned for her, she told him, "This nice lady is telling me about Jesus. You've got to come and listen too." By then Tony had arrived with our car. I actually didn't want our conversation to end and Tony joined in. I sensed the Lord's presence. The lady and her son left our company completely set free. The gospel is good news. It was the Holy Spirit that had drawn her to me. I was also strengthened by the experience.

# STEP 10—CELEBRATE, IT'S A NEW SEASON

## Vacilando

We live in an area that is surrounded by steep hills. As part of my daily walks, I would pace myself to climb the hill, nearest to my home, all the way to the top without stopping. At first I found it difficult, and had to rest several times, but I wouldn't give up. There was a sense of achievement each time I made it to the top. The more times I made the journey, the fitter I became. Soon I was able to climb the hill with ease. After a while it dawned on me how much I was enjoying the journey. From then on I could relax, take it all in and enjoy the scenic views around me. I welcomed the fact that the rest of the journey would be downhill all the way.

The peak is the highest part of a hill, where the ground starts to become flat. I made the connection that when you reach the peak of your life's challenges, you will know from then on, the journey will become easier.

*Vacilando* is a Spanish term that means to travel with the knowledge that the journey is more important than reaching the specific destination.

I remember the very first time we drove in the motor home to Spain. We went by ferry and then we drove from one end of Spain to the other. It seemed like an eternity to the children. They were excited and couldn't wait to get to the destination. At each interval, they would ask, *"Are we there yet?"*

I guess that's how each part of the journey has felt for me. In the same way, Father God reminded me that growing in relationship with Him was far more important than reaching the destination and everything I experienced along the journey was working together for my good and the good of others.

I compare this to the many years of struggling that people go through before they are healed. The miracle was instantaneous but the journey was arduous and long. I imagined how eager Jesus was to heal people who were ready to receive from Him.

Healing goes beyond a physical transformation. Jesus spoke the words "Thy faith has made you whole," to numerous people. One of these was the woman who had suffered from a haemorrhage for twelve years. Her victory came after years of struggles; the lack of resources, for she spent all that she had, yet her condition grew worse; the emotional, psychological and physical pain she endured; the torments of fear, intimidation and ostracism. She probably hadn't been physically touched by another human being, neither had she heard a kind word spoken towards her for 12 long years. She searched for her identity, but believed what others had called her—an outcast, a dropout from society, yet she persistently pressed through the crowd, the same people who had victimised and stereotyped her. We are not even told her name!

Then, she touched His garment. Immediately, something changed on the inside and impacted her whole being. Jesus affirmed her and called her, "Daughter, your faith has made you whole." I imagine she was whole in every sense of the word.

In the Bible, 'wholeness' is the state of being perfectly well in spirit, soul (our mind, will and emotions) and body.

Our salvation includes more than going to heaven, even though that's our eternal destination. In the Greek *salvation* is rendered as *deliverance from the penalty of sin and eternal separation from God*. It is also *deliverance from danger*. The term *sozo* is another word for salvation. It means *deliverance from danger or destruction, to be saved, to have protection, preservation, healing, restoration, soundness and wholeness*.

It is absolutely clear from scripture, that God isn't the one who puts disease, disaster and devastating situations on humanity. They originate from the evil one and are the result of disobedience to God's laws. But Jesus became a curse for us and has redeemed us from the curse of the law (Galatians 3:13). So why are believers, seemingly defeated and oppressed by the devil when we have been given authority and power over all the power of the enemy?

I remember a conversation I had with one of the bishops in our church. He had observed how both the believer and non-believer were facing the same challenges in their lives. He couldn't understand the reasons why. I understood where he was coming from, and I didn't know the answer myself. The facts were that believers were experiencing all kinds of defeats. It wasn't that we weren't experiencing the blessings of God, but they weren't the fullness of what we knew was available to us. We were seeing premature deaths, sicknesses, living in debt and lack and were experiencing all kinds of tragic events. Wasn't this a similar question that the Psalmist David asked God? Why were the wicked prospering? He soon got the answer when he searched for God.

Although we don't see the extremity of persecution for the sake of the gospel, as in other parts of the world, we still face trouble. In fact Jesus puts it this way—in this world you will have trouble. But notice, He told us to cheer up because we are overcomers! That's it. I am an overcomer and not a survivor.

> I am an overcomer and not a survivor.

To borrow a phrase from Creflo Dollar, I am the healed protecting my health.

We too must press through our doubt, fear and unbelief, until our faith is activated. Then we can experience all the blessings of wholeness, and impart them to others. Therefore, I consider that wholeness isn't the absence of trouble. It's how we respond when they arrive. When we know what to do and how to take authority in the face of adversity, we will not submit to oppositions that come against us. When we stand in Christ we cannot be defeated.

I believe we're living in the days where signs and wonders will be on a scale so great that it will become a way of life. I can hear the resounding words of Jesus to believers. Signs will follow those that believe.

Now I have found a better way. I no longer try to get my faith to work. Rather, I live a lifestyle of walking in faith.

Does God have a purpose in our setbacks? Absolutely, yes! The Cambridge dictionary defines 'setbacks' as *'Something that happens that delays or prevents a process from developing.'* In the general scheme of God's timetable, for the believer, setbacks are temporary events. They are springboards to take us to where we need to be; they give us the opportunity to change our present circumstances, and are designed to set us up for success. *"'But thanks be to God, who always leads us in triumph in Christ, and through us spreads and makes evident everywhere the sweet fragrance of the knowledge of Him.* 2 Corinthians 2:14. The lessons I have learnt along the way have far exceeded the challenges I've been through. Because of this I found that intimacy with the Father and doing what He says IS my number one priority. Becoming more like Jesus is my greatest achievement. I have learnt that with God, there are no limits to what He has for us. He has revealed Himself in ways I couldn't imagine or dream about. As long as I hunger and thirst for more of the Father, the Holy Spirit will lead me into a deep and intimate knowledge of Jesus.

I haven't arrived, but have come a long way from where I was, to where I am. As I look back over the events of 2016, I can see what the Lord has done and is doing in me. My attitude has changed towards life. I no longer take the smallest thing for granted. I appreciate and celebrate each moment, with thanksgiving. When I feel discouraged and want to give up, the Father reminds me of how far I've come. He's bringing me into wellness and wholeness, spirit soul and body. Each season has brought fresh hope. *"Hope deferred makes the heart sick, But when desire is fulfilled, it is a tree of life"* (Proverbs 13:12).

## Make the change happen

To help you make the decision, here are some important principles to consider. Change demands will-power, drive and motivation. It requires steadfastness and vision. But it starts from within you and not the other way round. You are only one decision away from making the change happen.

You are only one decision away from making the change happen.

For the believer, change flows out of a loving and intimate relationship with God. Watch how the Father lovingly corrects you, and masterfully remoulds and reshape you to become more and more like Him. Change happens over time and is an ongoing process.

All the Father requires is our submission to Him on a daily basis. I learnt that all I ever hope to achieve is in Him.

What are the changes you want to see in your life? Are you battling to lose weight? Do you want to have a healthier lifestyle? Do you want to lead a stress free life; to make the move to achieve a goal; leave a legacy for your loved ones or to write that book you've talked about?

The definition of insanity, is doing the same thing over and over again, but expecting a different result (Albert Einstein). If what you have been doing so far has not achieved the expected results, simply use a *different* approach from the one you were using before.

We are told by scientists that habits can be changed in 30 days, but it's a matter of changing the way we think. The Bible teaches, *'For as he thinks in his heart, so is he [in behaviour—one who manipulates]* (Proverbs 23:7). According to Dr. Caroline Leaf, the author of 'Who Switched off my Brain,' our thoughts stimulate our emotion, then attitude and behaviour. Science is proving what the Bible has taught us all along.

When I was serious about losing weight, my sister, Eil took me along to aerobics classes. I had to make sacrifices along the way. Losing weight was one of my priorities. At the time, it wasn't my idea of fun. I wasn't in the right frame of mind. When I changed my attitude, however, I realised that I was actually enjoying myself. I started with small steps. My goal was to lose weight but in the process, I became healthier and was more energised.

Diet and fitness became a part of my routine. Each day I would get up early at 6.00 am. After prayer and devotion, I would spend an hour exercising. I found that I had the energy to make breakfast, get the children washed and dressed for school and do a day's work. I was so motivated that I started an aerobics class. At that time, I was still pastoring the local church, so I introduced aerobics to the ladies. It took off rapidly. Soon, we set up our own ladies exercise classes. Colleagues, family and friends saw the benefits, and soon word had spread that I was educating others on lifestyle changes. Through this avenue, I received many referrals from the hospital's Occupational Health and word of mouth, to my programme on 'making healthy lifestyle changes.'

At last I found the key to change and applied the principles to my spiritual life, health and finances. My faith expanded and soon the Father gave me visions and dreams I had never experienced before. They were so instrumental in how I moved forward. God was indeed speaking to me in amazing ways.

Be consistent in the change you want to see happen. You may not be where you want to be right now but soon you will be on your way to victory. Taking small steps is better than gigantic leaps and finding out you are unable to maintain it.

When you immerse yourself in His unfailing love, you too can be victorious. You are an overcomer and more than a conquer. You can put your trust in the God who loves you and can never let you down. He will fulfil all He's started in you.

It's over one year since I had been given a few months to live. Since my CT scan in 2016 the tumours in my abdomen had increased. Tony and I started counting the number of tumours we could feel in my stomach, and stopped counting after we found there were 15.

Today they have all dissolved. I hold onto the scripture He gave me from the start of my journey. 'For yet a little while and the evil-doers will be no more' (Psalm 37:10). To check the patient's progress, doctors use the results from the patient's blood tests, tumour markers, scans and physical examinations.

My tumour markers have consistently decreased. On 13th June 2016 they were 300 u/ml. Soon they had decreased to 189.4 u/ml. Since the beginning of 2017, they are consistently undetectable—less than <5u/ml.

I continue to walk in divine health and declare healing over any symptoms that try to invade my body.

It's time to celebrate your new season. You too can live the life that God created you to live—prosperous, fearlessly, victoriously and triumphantly.

I AM healed, delivered and made whole.

"Now to Him who is able to [carry out His purpose and] do superabundantly more than all that we dare ask or think [infinitely beyond our greatest prayers, hopes, or dreams], according to His power that is at work within us, [21] to Him be the glory in the church and in Christ Jesus throughout all generations forever and ever. Amen" (Ephesians 3:20, 21).

# ADDENDUM

## Appendix 1

Interview with a consultant psychotherapist

## Appendix 2

A practical approach to develop good parenting strategies for
children with emotional and additional needs

## Appendix 3

Nutritional and juicing recipe tips to optimise nutritional health

# APPENDIX 1

## Richard Dowey (Consultant Psychotherapist) interviewed by Hyacinth Wheeler-Fraser, 30 March 2016, Interview 2 Transcript.

## Background

Tony and I were sitting together with Richard at his clinical practice, deliberating over the poor service we were still receiving. There had been several other times that we had spent hours, in our front room, having the same conversations. Much to our dismay, we ended up where we started, still fighting a system that had not changed for centuries.

The statutory governing bodies have now recognised that more could be done to address the inequalities and lack of resources available, to offer meaningful support to adoptive families. Evidently, there is a strong link that children and young people in the care system are many more times likely to become involved in the criminal justice system; less likely to achieve academically and unlikely to secure long term employment.

Richard, a former social worker, said how he felt a deep sense of shame to be associated with the Social Care organisation. He had witnessed how unfairly we had been treated. He was the only professional, involved with our case that had any scruples. He had become a trusted friend and was instrumental in helping us to fight our corner in a professional manner. Years after, he was commissioned by the local authority to provide therapeutic support for our children and ourselves. Although it was a step forward, it had taken many years to achieve and therapy for the children may have come all too late.

When I met up with Richard, he was willing to share his feelings as he had done on many occasions, but this time in an interview.

I wanted to know what he felt had gone so very wrong for our family. His choice of words and their intensity, suggested he genuinely empathised with our family. He had been on our journey and believed that the whole care system right back to the government was failing vulnerable young people and families, such as ours. He spoke deeply, carefully and passionately about what was, in his estimation, a contradiction in government policy: its effect was the erosion of certain parental rights, while expecting parents to accept responsibility for their children's actions.

He spoke about current legislation and described, what he felt were the effects of moving children in care, from one establishment to another depending on the Care Order they were under. Some of the examples he gave were:

**Richard:** Section 20 allows the local authority to accommodate children on a voluntary basis. This requires a signed agreement from the parents. Section 3 on the other hand is a Care Order where the local authority shares or takes the lead in parental responsibility. The age group for children in care has increased from 16 to 18. Depending on the Order, children are now classed as 'being in care' up to the age of 25.

The fact that the government has made it mandatory that all children and young people should stay in education until they are 18, forces them into higher education or to take up apprenticeships. Keeping young people in education longer is recognition that:

- Work is diminishing, which simply means that there is not enough work to go around

- The State wants to return responsibilities to the parents, but then these rights are taken away by certain rights of children. This presents as a massive contradiction and a conflict between the children's rights and parental responsibility.

There are certain restrictions being put on parental involvement in their children's lives. For example, 16 year olds' now have the freedom to withhold information from parents. This is reflected in the fact that:

- GPs will not disclose anything to parents, without the child's consent.
- Children can take their parents to court, yet if a child is in police custody, the parents are expected to attend as the appropriate adult. If they refuse, the police cast aspersions about the parents' commitment to the child.

The statistics regarding children in the care and the judicial systems are very high. The prospects of children and young people achieving academically before they leave school, and being able to secure a job or career of their choice, is significantly reduced. They are likely to end up in one of two routes—the criminal or judicial system and mental health services.

**Hyacinth: What is the link with mental health?**

**Richard:** It goes back to the ways in which children, who have been in the care system experience trauma. They develop certain mechanisms or strategies to cope with the trauma of being a 'Looked After Child', and all the experiences that goes along with that.

Typical scenarios are when a young person experiences:

- A number of changes in social work staff.
- A number of different placements, for example they are placed in a children's home and afterwards they end up going to two or more foster carers.

- If the young person was involved in criminal activity, there are additional adults who would be involved in their lives. For example, if the young person is in a secure unit, they would be allocated additional adults. As they grow older, they will have to cope with even more and different social work teams.

These young people have more relationships and engagement with the adults working with them than any other group of children. Rather than being with their peers, they are mainly in the company of adults. The reason why these children came into the Care system in the first place, is because of an absence of secure attachments, despite having strong bonds to their parents.

If a young person has been diagnosed with an avoidant or chaotic attachment, and they have had constant changes of the adults in their lives, that attachment style becomes entrenched and more acute. The young person then becomes more avoidant and more chaotic.

**Hyacinth: It's like a vicious circle?**

**Richard:** . . . that's right, and you may have a combination of the two, which then goes on to influence and impact the young person emotionally, psychologically and relationally. Emotionally is how you feel about yourself and others, psychologically is the way you think about yourself and feel about others. Relationally, in terms of quality and nature of the relationships you have with yourself and others. This affects your peers and those older than you, those who look like you and those who look different to you. It affects them all—so you become avoidant or you become chaotic in those relationships. You also become chaotic in your thoughts, avoidant in your feelings or chaotic with your feelings.

**Hyacinth: Why are we not prepared to address a system that's failing?**

**Richard:** There are two or three strands to your question.

Firstly, quite simply there's no 'money' to be gained out of 'feelings'. Cognitive Behaviour Therapy (CBT) is the same approach that the mental health unit, CAMHS uses. It's about how your cognitions affect behaviour. How your behaviour affects the way you think, moves you to act and whether those actions affect your daily functioning. It's a way of changing those things that get in the way of functioning as a responsible member of society. For example, having a job and paying taxes. The CBT approach works better for people who misuse alcohol or who have issues with weight or people who want to give up cigarettes. These are short term day to day stressors that most of us face in different ways across the course of our lives. We all struggle with phobias of all kinds, obsessions and compulsions at different times too.

Behind any obsession, compulsion or any habit-forming behaviour that leads to say overeating or misuse of alcohol or drugs, there will be a root cause. There is also a feeling that comes with the root cause. For example, what made someone take up smoking in the first place is one thing. What made an individual become addicted to the cigarettes is another. It's usually linked to some kind of experience that's happened to us in a relationship that is essentially traumatic and becomes at the very least, stressful or traumatic.

You then look at ways to remediate the stress. Some people go to drinking wine or eating chocolates, for example. Stress is ongoing, and you look for some way to alleviate the stress factor, using wine or chocolate, etc. It doesn't matter what age you are. Whether it's the baby in the pram or adults of any age, we learn to develop coping strategies to get our needs met. Babies find ways of attracting the attention of the significant caregiver. As you get older, it just becomes more and more sophisticated.

Firstly, there's an absence in society or an unwillingness to get in touch with the feelings behind some of the strains and stresses that we have. For example, if you work in the retailing industry employees are expected to work shift patterns to suit the consumer. But this is to the detriment of the employees. The impact on their emotions and relationships are often not thought about.

Secondly, there's no regard for people's beliefs and values which are both linked. There is a tendency when professionals, who work with families, make their own judgements. This is usually based on their life's experience and belief systems. Consequently, they tend to dismiss and test your values and beliefs, to the effect that this can impact on your self-esteem. We don't see how other people's views of us make us act, therefore we don't see or try to understand why a person may act the way that they do.

We have not necessarily understood why it is that Jenny, for example, acted or allowed her action to manifest by making the decision to get a tattoo. Nor do we necessarily appreciate, as professionals, the significance of Jenny having the tattoo on her face; how this affects her emotional, psychological and relational functioning and wellbeing in the here and now and into the future.

We reduce human beings generally to a two-dimensional sphere. If you are a child of colour, the reduction goes further or there are additional processes that reinforce or add to the diminution of self of the person, such as racism—that's what racism is designed to do. I don't normally use that term as it doesn't seem to make any difference and young people don't 'get it' these days, but when we talk about a shade, then they get that it's a 'shade based process'. I believe these 'differences' are designed to make you feel small or to make you think small about yourself and other people who look like you.

Sexism works in the same way. It is designed to make women feel small about themselves and other women, and to make men feel big and powerful. What happens when you don't feel like that? You're made to feel that way. People are pressurised into thinking themselves to be small or feel less than others. There are jobs that children of colour are expected to do such as singing, rapping, being an athlete or a dancer and so on (although not all Black people can dance.

I know some Black people that dance terribly), but we are made to feel like you ought to be able to do these things.

**Hyacinth: You mean stereotypical behaviour?**

Yes. Or when you don't look or behave or feel as the stereotype, then all sorts of things go on psychologically, emotionally or relationally. You don't know how to live in the world, to be like the world, but you're being told one thing—the options aren't wide or extended.

In the mid-1950s or earlier in certain parts of the country and up to the mid-1970s, people of colour weren't considered as members of the community who had recently migrated here. Straight away they were considered to be a part of the class system. Although they were a part of it, they didn't know it. There were quite a few children who were placed for adoptions in those times. There weren't any Black people adopting at that time, but there were a lots of White people.

When I became a social worker in the 1980s, and throughout the early 1980s, all of the evidence available was taken from these children, who were then becoming young adults. They were now ready to share their experiences of adoption. The information we have are from children of Colour, some who are Mixed Race. One young person shared the following story: 'I was sitting in the bath with the Vim and Brillo in my hands.'

Although they lived in affluent neighbourhoods, they were literally scrubbing off their skin. They were living with their parents in large houses of the country side. They had all the material things you could ever imagine. Despite them having all of these things, they were saying, 'This is what I did to myself because I was confused about who I was and the environment I lived in. All the information we were given from well-meaning people who wanted to adopt and provide homes for children similar to us, was to give us a good start.'

The experience they had affected their emotional, psychological and relational well-being. Most of the information I hear regularly, is similar to this experience. It points out that young Black people, who ended up in crime, were unable to secure jobs, because they didn't finish their education. They developed lots of psychological difficulties in their relationships because of the turmoil they were dealing with. Consequently, some of it meant that adoptive placements broke down."

**Hyacinth: Are you saying that a particular class of people who were living in affluent areas were the ones who were adopting Black children? Was the cause of adoption breakdown due to children who were unable to relate to their identity?**

**Richard:** Absolutely and neither were these children's identity supported by their adoptive parents.

**Hyacinth: So, why would they adopt Black children?**

**Richard:** At that time children were mainly adopted.

**Hyacinth: Looking at the challenges that we were up against, how should we parent children who obviously are suffering from post-traumatic stress disorders?**

**Richard:** You have to recognise that you are parenting traumatised children within a system which traumatises. I only now understand why our parents didn't allow us to go out and play. They were trying to protect us from something that only adults knew about.

(Richard went on to share about his first 'racist' experience, when he was a young 6-year-old child. He recalls how one of his school peers had used words to describe the way he had looked. From his recollection of the incident, he told me that he had learnt an important lesson about trauma. Although he didn't understand what the person had said to him at the time of the incident, he had 'felt' the racism that was coming from the person. Whenever he is put in a similar situation, he will disengage as part of his defence mechanism. He recalled how he still remembers how the incident had left him traumatised.

So, these are the kind of things we experience that inform the way that we relate. Furthermore, Looked After Children that have been in the Care system are prepared for adoption. It's also important to prepare their parents to understand the child and the differences and diversities that they would be bringing, even when the parents 'look' like them.

The differences and diversity that child is going to be bringing are not the same as you would bring because it's about the experience that you would have had. So it's how your children, Hyacinth (the experience of how they have been parented) fits in with their sense of identity and how that has come together to produce the children they are today. Once we have an understanding of this, we are then ready to unpack it. It's not just unpicking it as a story, but it's unpicking the story of the feelings in the story and the thinking behind it. So that's why what may have seemed insignificant to me when I was young, was actually significant because 50 years later it still has an impact on me today.

As human beings, we know how influential what we experience in our early years are real to us today. Particularly, when we take the time to sit down and talk about it we will realise how much of an impact they have had on us. We are trained to do this as social workers. As psychotherapists, psychologists and psychiatrists, we are all trained to do that, but somehow, when it comes to feelings and skin colour something starts to go wrong. Professionals either block out the feelings or refuse to see you as having different needs. Your difference does something to them. They either want to control or dismiss you as a person of colour. It's not necessarily about embracing you, or seeing you as 'my equal.' [Richard goes on to give an example of how stereotyping works from the perspective of a White European]. "My history as a White European is that I've been trained from very early to see the world like this—I'm up here and you're down there." This kind of perception is in the education system, it's in the media, and it's everywhere.

**Hyacinth: Does it come down to racism and inequalities?**

**Richard:** Yes, there's an inequality all the time from the moment you're conceived in this country. Even if you're born outside the country, when you arrive here you will be faced with it. It's already a part of the genetic code of people who are born here.

I wrote in my dissertation that when I hear the crack of the whip, my blood goes cold. While I have never had the experience, it is a certain sound. It is something that is generational. Our people were whipped to death. There are certain things that we carry in our DNA. We carry the experience, and that's the same as any kind of trauma.

When you look at neuroscience, it talks about the 'synaptic pathway development.' The trauma experienced within parental relationships characterised by, e.g. insecure/avoidant attachments, affects empathic awareness, growth, how a child gains attention from those parental relationships and is believed to affect neuro biological development.

The only way to make that happen, once a child has had the trauma, is for them to experience empathy and the experiences **they** need to enable the child to develop their empathy; otherwise they can't do it.

When we talk about ADHD, it means when you don't get enough attention, you kick off. A child may behave in desperate, intense and agitated ways in order to gain attention, with the child consciously and unconsciously acting out the learned/conditioned strategies to achieve their physical, emotional, relational and psychological needs. You become hyperactive. You know that if you do it long enough you get attention, albeit the wrong kind attention. It then becomes a disorder. It affects the way you function in society and the way society believes a person of your age should be functioning. The solution is to give those children the attention they need and the experiences they need.

When your children came to you Hyacinth at four and five-and-a-half years' old, they already had developmental deficits. There are things that they should have had that they didn't have. Somewhere in the course of their lives, those holes or gaps needed to be filled. They needed to have appreciation for things they experienced whenever they experienced them.

So within the system, we have looked at things that are against successful adoptions of people of colour or anyone caring for children of colour, because of the deficits they have.

I was recently speaking with a social worker and asked her about how she dealt with some of these significant issues. She discussed the issue of how the children's birth mother was not functioning, dad's absence and drug use. The plan was to send the grand-daughter to her grandfather, who is White British and lives in a White area. My question to her was 'what does the grandfather understand about differences and diversities? Does he understand it through the media for example? How does his next-door neighbour feel about his grand-daughter who is of Mixed parentage? Is he aware that he needs to be thinking about these things because his granddaughter is going to need his support? If he doesn't, then it's going to mess up the child, as she grows older not knowing her identity.

Back in the 1980s, it was not a good idea to have the same race placements because it wasn't the norm. Consequently, Black children were placed back in the Care system. Afterwards they began to look for Black adopters. Nowadays children are placed in trans-racial placements. Sometimes they are placed in a White family because it is better than having no family at all.

**Hyacinth: Why is it the case?**

We have even moved into getting the right colour and the right shade, so Social Care falls into the trap every time. They let their own anxieties, fears, and their own stereotypes affect their judgement. They allow their values and beliefs to get in the way of how adoption is supposed to work based upon the filter of race they have learned.

For Black children, the idea is that it is better to have this view of the world. They use the same approach to the reasons for breakdown, challenges and difficulties in foster and adoption placements. I hope you understand the link I've made.

In terms of providing a diagnosis for both Jason and Jenny based on my IC10 [a scale used by psychotherapists]. There are more than half a dozen specific disorders of which they are showing traits of. They range from post-traumatic to obsessive disorders of all kinds. On the autistic spectrum shades of depression, without a doubt, they would be considered bipolar (the old manic depression) of high mood and low mood. You see that with Jenny every day—one minute she is high, hyperactive even, another minute she is sullen and withdrawn. All of these are brought on by stresses, and the stresses of the experiences that they have had. We've all got them, but the question is what causes them to become more acute?

When I'm exposed to lots of different people, and feel as though I am put under pressure, my shyness as an example comes out. I can cope with it once. I may be able to cope with it today. One a month is fine, but if I have four within a month or four a day, stress builds up and that stress becomes anxiety. The anxiety could manifest itself as headaches. Sometimes I would swear or do other things to keep myself calm. That may mean taking a drink that night before to help me cope the following day. Then all of a sudden I would find that doesn't work and I have to have a little just before going out. Before you know it there's a habit going on. Soon it becomes a snow ball effect and I no longer can cope without alcohol. I become a hermit. It keeps me locked inside, and I'm afraid to go out.

As with my shyness, it means that I wouldn't go out anymore. Then I begin to do things such as locking all the windows. I would just sit there and start to hoard things such as newspapers and wouldn't want to talk to anybody. I would only talk to people through the letter box and then all of a sudden people who knew me, start looking at me as though something was wrong. If this continues, one day I might do something that is out of character for me or what people aren't expecting. Suddenly the psychiatric services would be called and off we go.

This scenario can be applied to food, chocolate, or anything that you like. These things are not bad in itself but it is how we use these things to help us to cope with the strains and stresses that we have.

So the best ways to parent your children are to engage with them through empathy; engage with genuineness and authenticity. Children know when you are not genuine, particularly, 'Looked After Children', who can spot it a mile off.

At the same time it is also important to look after yourself. We are not encouraged to learn about ourselves and to be empathetic with each other. Our Society doesn't encourage us to take responsibility for ourselves. We are not taught how to be empathetic with others. There's more emphasis about going out there and earning a living; making sure you have material things because more value is placed on material things. We learn to gain acceptance by others through this system. It's only when people show they are valued by each other, that's when they will be able to converse in the right manner with one another.

# APPENDIX 2

## A PRACTICAL APPROACH TO DEVELOP GOOD PARENTING STRATEGIES FOR CHILDREN WITH EMOTIONAL AND ADDITIONAL NEEDS

While this guide is based on our experience of parenting children with emotional and additional needs, this section does not in any way constitute a comprehensive guide or any expertise in this field. Therefore, it is advisable that professional help is sought for your child who may display these needs. There is much literature and books on the subject that are available through the internet and specific websites. However, a good GP is your first port of call. He will assist you in making the necessary referrals.

Special educational needs and disabilities affect a child or young person's ability to learn. Our children's behavioural issues affected their ability to socialise. For example, they found it difficult to keep the friendships they formed. Jason is academically gifted. Jenny's main difficulties are in numeracy and literacy. They both have short concentration spans.

As a result of his behavioural challenges and poor social skills, our local educational psychologist referred our son for an education statement. The statement of education described his emotional needs and allowed him to have additional support in school and further education. We found that appropriate resources were either unavailable, limited or of poor quality. The statement was kept on his file and followed him throughout his education.

Through our persistency, the children were eventually diagnosed with Attention Deficit Hyperactivity Disorder, several years apart. The symptoms displayed in their behaviours were inattentiveness, hyperactivity, and impulsiveness. The symptoms were related to early years of traumatic upbringing, attachment issues, and ongoing life experiences. The diagnoses were given by the psychotherapist and community paediatrician. At the time when medication was recommended, our son was at the age where he was given the choice by social workers, and he chose not to take it.

Our son was a gifted child and avid reader. However, his short attention span landed him into difficulties at school and in social settings; he was easily distracted and influenced by others. On the other hand, our daughter excelled at sports, especially football but didn't have the discipline to fully commit herself to the task. Reading and writing were hard, but her photogenic memory assisted her to the degree it went unnoticed that she was borderline dyslexic. She found it harder to comprehend the meanings of words. Numbers and instructions are confusing and have to be broken down to assist her.

At the start of teenage years, the huge problem for us was the amount of risk they took. They had little or no sense of danger. They didn't learn from past mistakes and the consequences of their actions and these actions have led well into their teenage years.

Underachievement at school, poor social interaction with other children and adults, and problems with discipline are symptoms that can cause significant problems in a child's life.

## Strategies

Children are angry and upset for many reasons but do not have the maturity or control to behave responsibly. Impulsiveness is hard to manage due to the underdevelopment of the brain. We came to the realisation that memories or hurts from the past often triggered emotional reactions, manifested in the way they behaved.

For example, if we gave an instruction they didn't like, or when they fell out with each other, I learnt to remain calm or walk away from the situation. This was time out for me. A time of reflection often changed the way I responded. I was able to deal with the situation in a more constructive way.

When the children told me about the flashbacks they were having, throwing tantrums to get their own way was far easier. I found the strategy of describing how they felt, even when they couldn't articulate it with words, gave me some indication.

More recently Jenny is able to warn me when she feels I'm 'lecturing her,' and it is becoming too much. I respond to her needs by saying, 'Okay, I can see this isn't helping.' It gives her the space and time she needs to regroup and stops her from reacting inappropriately. On occasions when she has been disrespectful towards me, she apologises. I capitalise on this time to improve our relationship with each other.

## Discipline to help develop good behavioural and organisational skills

Setting firm, clear boundaries and being consistent in your parenting strategy are key to discipline. It works well when both parents are committed and in agreement. Any disagreements should be discussed away from the children; otherwise, this will cause conflict in the home. We noticed how quickly the children were able to pick up on this, and tended to play one parent off against the other.

## Reward Charts

Reward charts are helpful for younger children. We first tried this strategy through the Tripple P Programme. Our children were between the ages of five and up to 12 years' old.

Setting the right rules or goals for your child is helpful. However, we found they were more committed to the rules if they were involved.

It gives the children a sense of responsibility and in any case, is much more fun. Keep the goals to a minimum of three or four; at the most up to six. The goals were based on the children's behaviour in school, home and social events.

A goal might be to keep tidy rooms. We agreed the details together. For example, they helped me to label where each item belonged. When things are not in its place, my children found it confusing. Equally, they found it challenging to keep their rooms tidy. They had previously got used to living in a house where piles of clothes and rubbish were kept.

The children were involved in agreeing the process of what the consequences and rewards were for each goal. A consequence might simply mean they didn't earn pocket money that week. The benefits of rewarding the children got them into a routine and they were able to earn pocket money. This strategy is still a good motivator.

## Timeout

As the children got older, we explored strategies that worked or didn't work as the case may be. For 'time out' the children were sent to stand at the door or go to their bedroom.

The recommended guidance for using time out is to multiply one minute for the age of the child. For example, if your child is five years old time out would last for five minutes. Time out may work up to twelve.

At the time when Jason was still in mainstream primary school, there were many times, when we were called to a meeting, Jason was sitting outside the head teacher's door. Isolation from the other children was a regular feature for Jason which ultimately led to several weeks of exclusion. In class, Jason was made to sit at the front or back of the class. When funding ran out, the qualified mentor working with Jason left. Jason was given an unqualified and inexperienced mentor to shadow everywhere he went in school. This was very frustrating for him, and he disliked the mentor because of this.

I am aware that time has moved on in mainstream school and there is much more integration for children with additional needs than before. Ask your social worker to support you with how school manages behaviour when the child is in school.

## Counting Technique

When your child knows how to meet an agreed instruction but is unwilling, this technique provides an opportunity for the child to reflect and act.

- Consistency is important. For example, if you say you will count up to 10, keep to it.
- Remind the child of the consequences. It gives them the opportunity to think through the expected action and outcome

When Jason was about 7 years old, there was a fall out with his sister. He resorted to hitting her and taking away her toy. When he refused to return the toy, I told him I would count up to 10 to give him the opportunity to return the toy, otherwise he would be sent to his room. When I got to 5, I told him to get to his room. I was alarmed when in tears he told me, "but you didn't count to 10." From this experience, I learnt that my own actions were inconsistent. I did apologise to Jason.

When I shared the story with a former social worker, he told me: *'it made me think about order and predictability; how our sense of security is found in the way that gives us a general sense of temporal order of things. We are all most anxious when we are unable to predict what happens next. The inability to predict leaves us unable to plan. Much of what we know about children who have had early traumatic experiences tells us that their levels of anxiety and stress are often considerably higher. They become dysregulated by incidents that other children might well be able to take in their stride.'*

## Coloured Cards

This technique was helpful in school and home. It helps your child identify feelings that can lead to express anger in a safe way. The child and adults working with them are aware of the meaning of the colours. For example, yellow, orange and red were the colours Jason used to express the way he was feeling. If he held up yellow card, for instance, the teacher would know he was uncomfortable about something. He rarely got the chance to raise a red card, because by that time his behaviour deteriorated.

## Giving Praise

Generally, giving constructive feedback is a good motivator, particularly when it is given with sincerity. Children and young people with emotional needs are skilful to differentiate when there is a lack of sincerity.

Praise should be given soon after the child has done something positive. It reinforces good behaviour and sends a clear message that the child's action was positive. It makes them feel appreciated and valued, and it feels good. I remember the smile of satisfaction on their faces when they heard the words: "well done" or "I'm very proud of you for doing that."

## The Importance of Therapy

### Ongoing assessments

When children have been in the Care system, we believe it is imperative that parents ask for ongoing assessments of their needs as they grow older. It is ironic that the assessment is referred to as *children in need of services*, yet when we ask for the services, they are not available. One social worker wanted to know why we had asked for assessments of the children, as in their mind there was nothing wrong with them. We knew differently. We didn't know if this approach was due to a lack of resources. However, therapeutic assessment should have been in place as part of the children's care package.

Over time the needs of children change, especially when they reach puberty. When they were stressed, we witnessed more aggressive and violent behaviours. Studies show that the brain develops functionally and structurally during adolescence, but these studies were defined by chronological age. Emotionally, our children were younger than their chronological age. The Care system failed to see the importance of therapy and gave them the choice. At that time, they chose not to have therapy because they were emotionally unable to make an informed choice. Now they are older they are finding their way towards realising they need some kind of therapeutic support to help them cope with day to day living.

## *Observation*

Observing your child's behaviour is important. It helps you to understand what can trigger unhealthy anger. Reflect and make a note of the following points:

> Aim: To help your child identify feelings when they are angry and discuss together strategies to help them prevent anger or use calming strategies

Question 1—What factors make your child angry?

_____

_____

_____

Question 2—Help your child describe how they felt before and after the incident?

_____

_____

_____

Question 3—Is the behaviour in school, home or at a social event?

_____

_____

_____

Question 4—How often does the behaviour occur—for example how many times per day, week or specific times? Is there a pattern?

_____

_____

_____

_____

_____

_____

Reflection—What are the learning points from the exercise? (Things to avoid such as diet or what to avoid such as negative approach or feedback). 'A soft answer turns away wrath.'

_____

_____

_____

_____

_____

_____

_____

_____

_____

_____

_____

_____

_____

_____

# APPENDIX 3

## NUTRITIONAL AND JUICING RECIPE TIPS TO OPTIMIZE NUTRITIONAL HEALTH

The phrase, 'you are what you eat', was derived from the belief that food controls our health. I personally found this to be true. When I arrived home from a busy day at work, it was easier to grab hold of a biscuit (or several) while I was cooking the evening meal. This was a habit I had formed over a period of time but I no longer do. Instead I snack on things that are healthier such as nuts or fruits.

Today the trend is to spend more on eating out at restaurants, cafes, and food courts, and consume fast and processed foods. Having a takeaway meal costs far more than buying groceries. Why is this, the new norm? It's probably due to how much time we have. There's nothing wrong with having a treat now and then, but do we really know what's in our foods?

Processed food is a term that applies to any food that has been altered from its natural state in some way either for safety reasons or convenience. They come in various forms.[6] They are ready-made meals that you can pop into the microwave or cook from frozen. It is important to understand how food labels work. Food labelled as 'use by date' is about safety and 'best before date' is about quality. In many cases, anything that has been processed contains added salt, sugar, and fat.

Our modern way of life has created pollution in the air we breathe and chemicals used to protect our food, has become more toxic, all of which affects our health. Our society is more concerned about making profit than they are about our health. That's one of the reasons why I use organic vegetables, wild fish (not farmed) and organic poultry. Organic food items are more expensive but it's the price I pay to protect my health and that of my family. There's a great investment in growing your own produce. It's cheaper and gives a sense of achievement when you eat your own produce.

In the next section I share some information about food and their nutrition to help you understand the benefits. Getting and staying well are a combination of nutrition, diet and exercise.

If you have serious health problems, however, please seek advice from health professionals regarding dietary requirements.

## What is nutrition?

Nutrition is about the study of food at work in our bodies; our source for energy and the medium through which our nutrients can function. Good nutrition means getting the right amount of nutrients from healthy foods in the right combination. I would also add that the right absorption levels are equally important. Eating right in terms of quality, amount, and having nutrients such as carbohydrates, proteins, and lipids (fats) as nutrition is one key to developing and maintaining good health. (What is Nutrition? 2001)

Having good health is defined as a state of complete spiritual, mental, physical, and social well-being. It is to maintain a healthy spirit, mind and body. Advice and information about our health are constantly changing but thank God that He is consistent in His plans for health and well-being.

Holy Communion or 'Lord Supper' is a special time when we remember the gruesome way in which Jesus suffered and died on the cross for us. His body was broken to bring healing, wellness and wholeness, and His blood was shed for our redemption. I believe that taking communion on a regular basis, optimises our wellbeing. In fact, God designed communion for healing and to maintain our supernatural health. For the believer, taking communion brings LIFE to every area of our lives (John 6:51).

## What is anti-oxidant?

*The word anti means against, and oxidants refer to oxidation meaning that antioxidants are substances that prevent cell damage caused by oxidation in the body. When certain types of oxygen molecules are allowed to float freely in the body, it can cause oxidative damage, which creates what is known as free radicals* (Roberts 2016).

Foods that are high in antioxidants are also considered cancer fighting foods.

They include garlic, broccoli, cabbage, cauliflower, sprouts and kale; shiitake mushroom, lemons and avocados.

- **Garlic** has immune-enhancing allium compounds that may help increase the activity of immune cells that fight cancer

- **Broccoli, cabbage, cauliflower, sprouts,** and **kale** contain antioxidants that may help to decrease cancer

- **Shiitake mushroom** contains powerful compounds that help in building immunity

- **Lemons** contain limonene stimulates cancer-killing immune cells. I regularly use lemons in cold and hot drinks, salad dressing and even use as a face pack with other ingredients

- **Avocados** contain powerful antioxidants that attack free radicals in the body by blocking intestinal absorption of certain fats

## The Immune System

Learning about the immune system and following a good nutritional diet, were the first things I did. Good health starts with maintaining a strong immune system. Father God created the immune system as an incredible defence mechanism to fight against bacteria, microbes, viruses, toxins and parasites, which can invade your body.

When the immune system isn't working properly, it causes all kinds of human ailments. For example—

*Allergies are a condition when the Immune system overreacts to certain stimuli that other people don't react to at all. Some people have diabetes, which is caused by the immune system inappropriately attacking cells in the pancreas and destroying them.* (Brain 2000)

The quality of our food has declined because our soil is not as good as it used to be. We are forced to eat Genetically Modified (GM) food, simply because there is a lack of clear labelling in our supermarkets.

Owing to the toxicity and quality in the foods we eat, supplementing our diets with the right supplements and vitamins, is advisable.

Having gone through cancer treatment there were times when my white blood cells and haemoglobin levels were low. As a result, I experienced a deficiency in iron and Vitamin B12. I take supplements to build my immune system, as directed by my doctor in integrative medicine.

As a patient of integrative medicine, my diet is based on raw and slightly cooked organic vegetables and green juice, where possible. We mainly buy organic produce. I've cut out most dairy products but eat organic eggs.

My new diet has a range of colourful vegetables, such as; beans and legumes, nuts and salads, whole and unrefined grains, gluten, yeast-free dairy and sugar-free bread, pasta and fruits.

Coconut oil and olive oil are healthier options. While I will use coconut oil because it is designed for cooking or frying at higher temperatures, for my salads, I mainly use organic olive oil.

A typical day for me would be to start the day with a mug of warm/ hot water with a slice of lemon, one garlic, and ¼ peeled ginger.

## Breakfast

I drink up to three cups of organic green tea (green tea can be counted towards your eight glasses of filtered water)

- I dissolve one mineral tablet in filtered water and drink, or
- A glass of filtered water with a teaspoon of bicarbonate of soda to alkalise the body
- A bowl of organic oats porridge made with almond or coconut milk, or
- A soft boiled organic egg with half a grapefruit
- Two to four glasses of green juice throughout the day to rehydrate the body

## Lunch

- Fruit bowl made up of blueberries, blackberries, one kiwi fruit, raspberries, papayas, ½ green apple (peel if not organic) and ¼ grapefruit (pink)
- A bowl of vegetable soup or lentil soup (chick peas or lentils) with butternut squash and other vegetables, and a slice or two of gluten free brown bread

## Evening

- Salad or brown rice with raw or slightly steamed vegetables, fish or chicken

## Juicing Recipies

### *Green juices*

I tend to use any greens I have at the time and use organic produce where possible. To wash the produce, I use filtered water, a dash of organic apple cider and half of squeezed lemon juice. Soak items for a few minutes and shake off/dry before juicing.

- 2 stalks of celery (celery makes a lot of juice), 1 whole cucumber, (peeled if not organic), broccoli, a cabbage leaf, handful of kale, 2 carrots and 1 garlic. Put all through the juicer.

### *Soursop milk shake*

**Soursop** is the fruit of *Annona muricata*, a broadleaf, flowering, evergreen tree. It is a native of the rainforests of Africa; the Caribbean; North and South America and Southeast Asia. Its edible white pulp can be eaten as a fruit or used as a milk shake. You will need a blender for this.

- A medium size fruit can make three or four glasses.
- Peel and de-seed the sour soup

- Add water or almond/coconut milk with a splash of lemon or lime

- Add a handful of seeds and nuts. It's thick and creamy consistency can be eaten as a yoghurt.

## Useful tips

### *The importance of drinking water*

Drinking clean, pure, water daily is a consistent message we've been hearing over the years, but we may not know the reasons why it is so important to our bodies.

According to an article, by Kathleen M Zelman, our body composition of water varies according to gender, age, and fitness levels because fatty tissue contains less water than lean tissue. On average the amount of water we have in our bodies ranges from 50-75%. The average adult human body is 50-65% water. The percentage of water in infants is much higher, typically around 75-78% water and dropping to 65% by one year of age.

When we lose fluid from our bodies through skin evaporation, breathing, urine and stools, it must be replaced daily. Our bodies know when we are dehydrated. After having treatments, I especially noticed how dehydrated I was.

Personally, I prefer filtered to tap water. When we eat out, I have mineral, sparkling or still water. When you buy water in the supermarket, it's better to buy water that is in glass bottles. Labelling of bottled water should include 'use by dates' as any other food or drink item.

I drink up to 2 litres of water daily. I drink more water during the day than the evening. Otherwise, you find that you're backwards and forwards to the bathroom at bed time.

*Where exactly is water in the human body?*

We are more water than we can image. Two-thirds (2/3) of the body's water is in the intracellular fluid. The other third (1/3) is in the extracellular fluid.

The amount of water varies, depending on the organ. Much of the water is in blood plasma (20% of the body's total). According to a study performed by H.H. Mitchell, and published in the *Journal of Biological Chemistry*, the following organs are comprised of these percentages of water: the human heart and brain—73%; the lungs—83%; muscles and kidneys—79%; the skin—64% and the bones—around 31% (Kathleen M Zelman 2016).

During treatment, I was extremely constipated. The side effect of taking certain medications for constipation was—Yes. You've got it—constipation! This was a vicious cycle. However, my doctors at Oasis of Hope advised me to drink more water, and it really helped. The advantages of drinking fluids (essentially water) are:

- It flushes out waste and toxins from the body, via the urine
- It helps to digest carbohydrates and is an aid in swallowing food
- It lubricates joints

*The importance of combining activity with diet*

Combining physical activity with diet can help us to reach and maintain a healthy weight, and reduce the risk of many health problems. Exercising is an important part of leading a healthy lifestyle.

Often health problems are related to the lack of exercise and being overweight. When you have found the right kind of exercise that is suitable for your needs, remember consistency is an important factor. Over the years I have enjoyed doing aerobics on my own with a video or in a group. I currently take short or long brisk walks, depending on the time I have, and have found it more suited to my lifestyle.

Swimming is also a great 'all-rounder' form of exercise to tone all of the muscles.

Over the last several months, it has been enormously challenging to get 8 hours sleep. This was due to the insomnia and tinnitus I had, even though I used both natural remedy and prescription drugs to help. Praise God I no longer need prescriptive drugs. I have found a combination of using lavender oils and bath salts in my bath, exercising during the day and reducing stresses in my life. I wish you every success in your choice of exercise.

# ENDNOTES

1. Lewis, C.S.

2. Inspirational Quotes: https://www.values.com

3. Bird's Eye View Images:

   https://www.bing.com/images/search?view=detailV2&ccid
   =cLNkI1g5&id=E9A9E8F79EA2A94A777244FFB
   38EA05D94B476EB&thid=OIP.cLNkI1g5Q8GIWJ
   es51DllAEsDh&q=Birds+eye+view+images&simid=
   608012554272113982&selectedIndex=28

4. Johari Windows: https://wwwbusinessballs.com

5. Contrearas, Francisco. *Health in the 21st Century* (Chula Vista,
   CA 91912, USA) Interpacific Press, February 1997

6. Live Well/Good Food: http://www.nhs.uk/Livewell/Goodfood/
   Pages/what-are-processed-foods.aspx

# BIBLIOGRAPHY

Archives, The National. *The National Archives.* www.nationalarchives.gov.uk (accessed June 30th, 2015).

*BBC.co.uk Science.* 19th April 2013. http://www.bbc.co.uk/science/0/21685448 (accessed June 30th, 2016).

Brain, Marshall. *How Your Immune System Works.* 1st April 2000. http://health.howstuffworks.com/human-body/systems/immune/immune-system1.htm (accessed July 31st, 2017).

Contreras, Francisco. *Health in the 21st Century.* Chula Vista, California 91912: Interpacific Press, 1997.

Dictionaries, Oxford Living. https://en.oxforddictionaries.com (accessed June 30th, 2016).

Dr. D. Glaser, Consultant Paediatric Psychiatrist, Great Ormand Street Hospital). *Understanding Attchment Difficulties, Joint Advice from the National Association of Head Teachers and Adoption UK.* https://www.adoptionuk.org/sites/default/files/Understanding-Attachment-Difficulties-flyer.pdf (accessed May 30th, 2017).

Foundation, Lockman. *Bible Gateway.com.* 2015; 1987. www.biblegateway.com (accessed June 30th, 2017).

—. *Biblegateway.* 2015; 1987. https://www.biblegateway.com (accessed June 30th, 2017).

Justin Machacek, Andi Kimbrough. *Reflections Promotional Spot.* Produced by Daystar Television Network. 2010.

Kathleen M Zelman, MPH, RD, LD. *6 Reasons to Drink Water.* 2nd November 2016. http://www.webmd.com/diet/features/6-reasons-to-drink-water#1 (accessed June 1st, 2017).

Luff, Ingham & (Alan Chapman adaptation, review and Code 1995-2014 based on Ingham & Luff's original Johari Windown concept. *Business.com.* 2017. http://www.businessballs.com/johariwindowmodel.htm (accessed May 30th, 2017).

Melinda Smith, Lawrence Robinson, Jean Segal. *Helpguide.org.* 30th April 2017. https://www.helpguide.org/articles/grief/coping-with-grief-and-loss.htm#resources (accessed March 133th, 2017).

Munroe, Myles. "Understanding Your Potential." In *Understanding Your Potential, Discovering the Hidden You*, by 1. Myles Munroe. Destiny Image, Publishers, Inc., Revised Edition 2002,2005.

Roberts, Catherine. *Nutrition and antioxidants.* 1st June 2016. http://www.activebeat.com/diet-nutrition/antioxidants-what-are-they-and-where-can-you-get-them/2/ (accessed May 17th, 2017).

UK, Adoption. *Understanding Attachment Difficulties.* (accessed June 30th, 2017).

UK, Cancer Research. *Cancer Research UK.* Name of publication, Cancer Research UK Cancer Research UK ([year of publication]). http://www.cancerresearchuk.org/health-professional/cancer-statistics/statistics-by-cancer-type/breast-cancer/incidence-invasive (accessed June 30th, 2017).

*What is a Journey.* Daystar, 2015.

*What is Nutrition?* 01 October 2001. http://whatisnutritiontips.com/ (accessed May 01, 2017).

Wikipedia. *https://en.m.wikipedia.org.* https://en.m.wikipedia.org (accessed June 30th, 2016).

# ABOUT THE AUTHOR

Hyacinth Wheeler-Fraser is author, entrepreneur and teacher. She is passionate about helping people to reach their potential and walk in their God-given purpose. She writes and delivers bespoke training and mentorship programmes to empower, inspire and mobilise people into action. Hyacinth has 40 years' experience in leadership and management positions in the church, corporate and voluntary sectors. She is a licensed Minister of Religion, educated to a Master's Degree in Strategic Management and Leadership. Hyacinth has been married to her best friend, Tony, for 35 years and they have two teenage children.